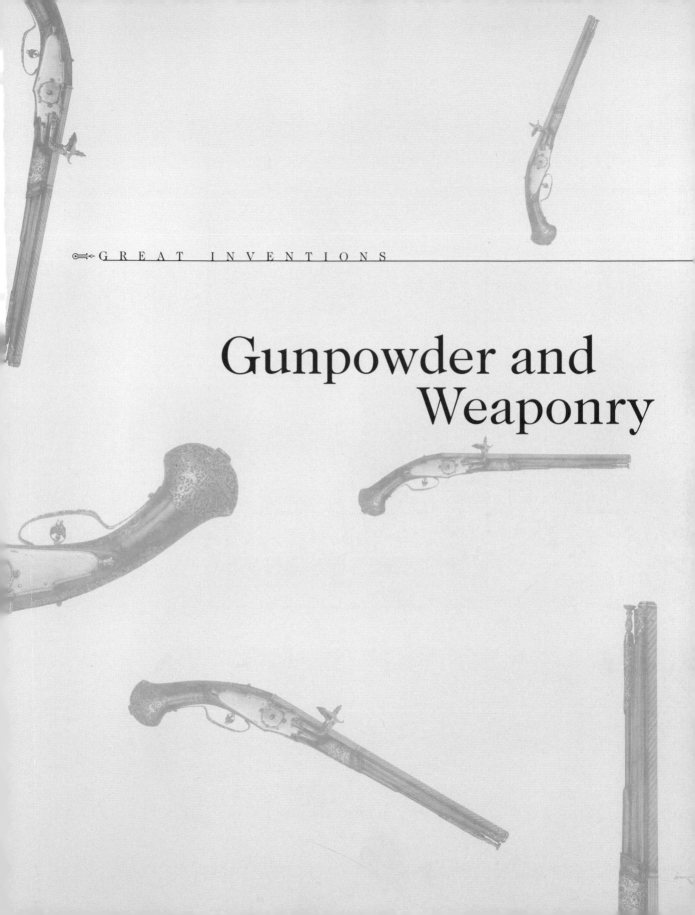

Gunpowder and Weaponry

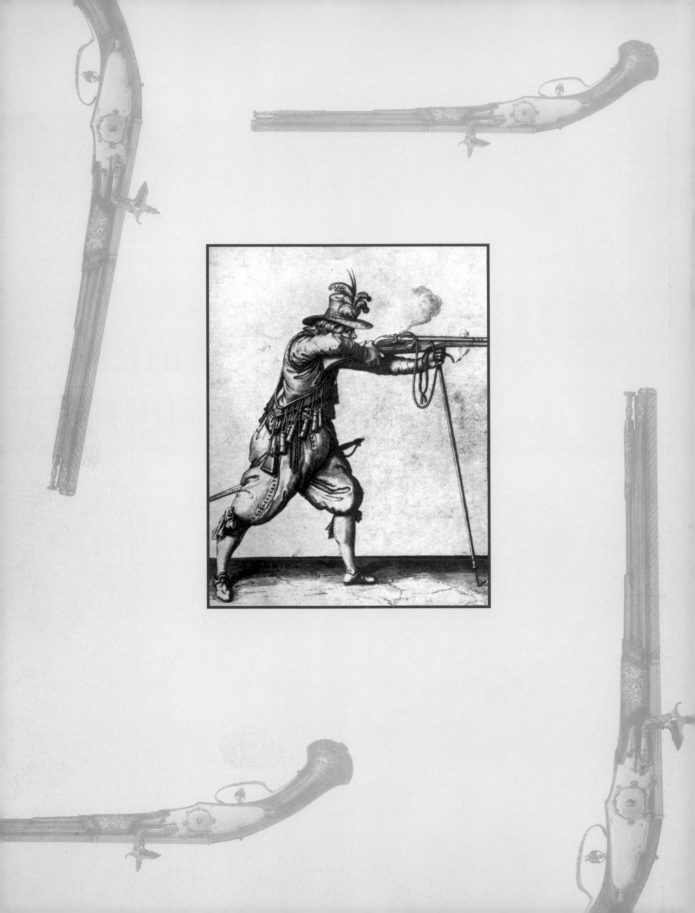

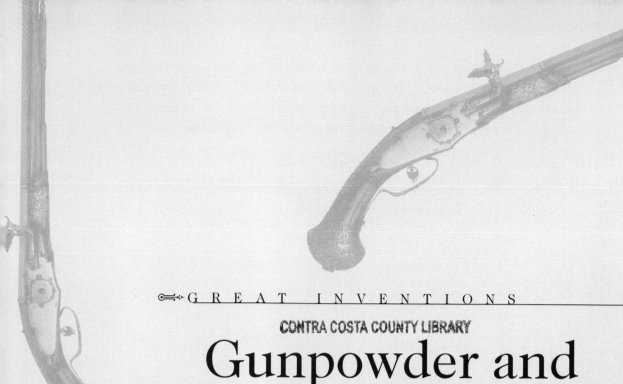

GREAT INVENTIONS

Gunpowder and Weaponry

JAMES LINCOLN COLLIER

BENCHMARK BOOKS

MARSHALL CAVENDISH
NEW YORK

The author would like to thank Dennis Showalter, professor of history, Colorado College, for his careful reading of the text. The book has been much improved by his comments and suggestions. However, the author is solely responsible for opinions and errors that may appear.

⚬━‹‹

Benchmark Books
Marshall Cavendish
99 White Plains Road
Tarrytown, NY 10591-9001
www.marshallcavendish.com

Text copyright © 2004 by James Lincoln Collier

Library of Congress Cataloging-in-Publication Data

Collier, James Lincoln, 1928–
Gunpowder and weaponry / James Lincoln Collier.
v. cm. — (Great inventions)
Includes bibliographical references and index.
Contents: Warfare before gunpowder — Gunpowder changes the ways of war
— The rise of the professional army — Europeans export their weapons
— The beginnings of the modern army — The Industrial Revolution in
weapons — The bloody century — What does it all mean?

ISBN 0-7614-1540-8

1. Military art and science—History—Juvenile literature. 2.
Gunpowder—History—Juvenile literature. 3. Ordnance—History—Juvenile
literature. 4. Firearms—History—Juvenile literature. [1. Military art
and science—History. 2. Gunpowder—History. 3. Ordnance—History. 4.
Firearms—History. 5. Weapons—History.] I. Title. II. Series: Great
inventions (Benchmark Books (Firm))

U39.C64 2004
623.4'526—dc21
2002156289

Photo research by James Lincoln Collier

Series design by Sonia Chaghatzbanian

Cover photo: Corbis/Philadelphia Museum of Art

The photographs in this book are used by permission and through the courtesy of:
New York Public Library: title page, 8, 11, 19, 27, 30, 33, 47, 75, 77. *Corbis*: 73, 91; Kevin Schafer,
14; Charles and Josette Lenars, 17; Ted Spiegel, 20; Dave Bartruff, 34; Philadelphia Museum of Art,
2, 20; Peter Johnson, 42; Historical Picture Archive, 44; Adam Woolfitt, 58; Bettmann, 48, 70, 89, 92.
Library of Congress: 54, 57, 61, 63, 80, 82-83, 86, 89. *The Jamestown Foundation*: 67.
Military History Archive: 96, 99, 105, 106, 109, 111, 116-117

Printed in China

135642

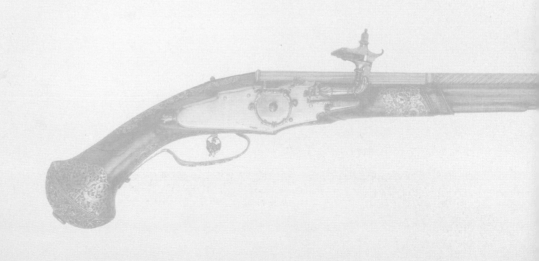

C O N T E N T S

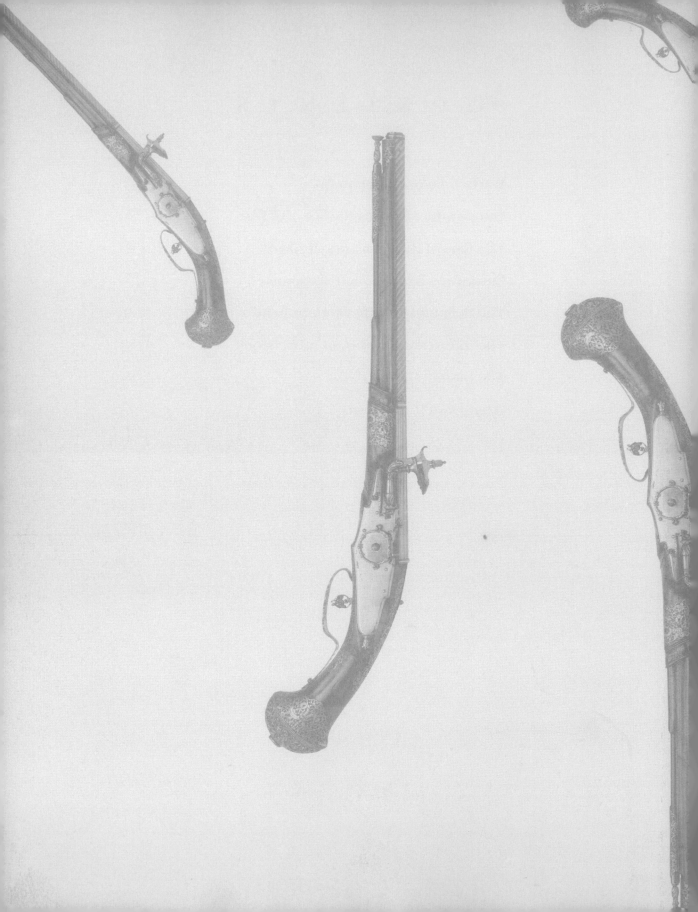

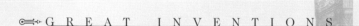

Gunpowder and Weaponry

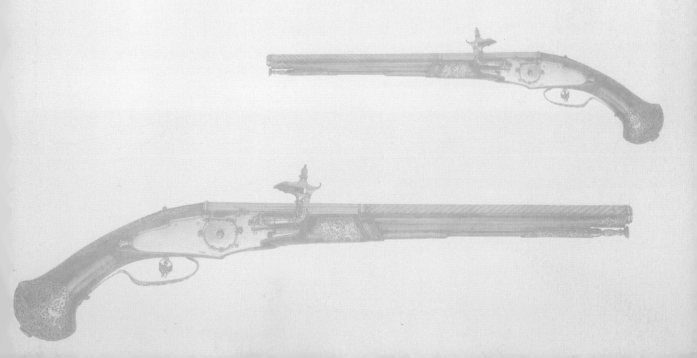

FIGHTING, IF NOT ACTUAL WARFARE, IS PROBABLY AS OLD AS HUMAN LIFE. THIS CAVE DRAWING FROM SPAIN, INSCRIBED IN THE DAYS WHEN HUMANS STILL LIVED IN SMALL HUNTER-GATHERER SOCIETIES, SHOWS BOWS AND ARROWS BEING USED FOR BOTH HUNTING AND WAR.

ONE

Warfare Before Gunpowder

Few inventions have had so profound an effect on the fate of nations as gunpowder. Within a hundred years after the first practical gunpowder weapons were developed, the nature of war was irrevocably altered. In another hundred years the people who were responsible for the creation of this powerful and terrifying new weapon had begun to dominate the world in a way that continues to the present day. To support the new style of warfare, new industries came into being. Not only did nations change, but the very idea of a nation was, at least in part, a result of the train of events that began with the development of gunpowder weapons. Gunpowder, indeed, changed the world.

Gunpowder and other explosives are not just used for war. Without explosives the foundations for modern buildings, modern roads, railroads, bridges, and much else would have been much harder, in some cases impossible, to construct. Explosives have been important to mining, and without them the Panama Canal could never have been dug. Indeed, gunpowder itself vastly increased humans' ability to hunt game, crucial to the early settlement of the Americas among other things. But the primary use of gunpowder, as the name itself suggests, has been for weapons of war.

War has almost certainly been a part of human life since humans have existed. In fact, war preceded humans: colonies of ants and other insects battled each other, and it came as a great shock to zoologists when the primatologist

9

Jane Goodall discovered two groups of chimpanzees she was studying, which she had assumed were peaceable, battling each other until the males of the smaller group were wiped out. But few species fight among themselves as relentlessly and viciously as human beings.

Early humans lived in small groups of varying sizes but probably most commonly containing between twenty and forty individuals. As a rule they wandered through a specified territory in search of fruit, berries, grains, eggs, small game, and occasionally larger animals such as mammoths. Although we do not know for certain that these early humans fought formal wars, injuries to fossil bones show clearly enough that there was fighting among them. Most likely, these little bands fought for rights to good campsites by lakes, for females, and for food sources. The earliest humans threw sticks and stones. Later groups developed increasingly better chopping and slicing tools made of wood, bone, and stone for hunting, for butchering the kill, and for war. By at least 25,000 years ago, particularly in what is now Europe, these small bands had created a large kit of wood, stone, and bone tools, often quite elaborately decorated. They painted the famous cave pictures, danced, made music, held religious ceremonies—and fought with each other.

About 10,000 years ago there was a change critically important to human life. Where the nomadic bands had once followed herds of animals in order to slaughter them as needed, they now began herding them. Where bands of people had once harvested wild grasses, fruits, and nuts, they began cultivating them. People were turning from hunting and gathering their food to farming it. This Neolithic revolution (*Neolithic* means "new stone age") altered life tremendously. A farmer could no longer wander, but had to settle down near his gardens and pastures. Small settlements sprang up. People could now store food—grain, honey, dried meat, dried fruit, and much else—for times of shortage. To do so they needed baskets and pots, which nomads would have found awkward to travel with. Weaving and pottery developed. Rough shelters turned into huts, huts into more permanent dwellings of leather, thatch, and poles. In time these Neolithic peoples learned to produce metal from ore to make ornaments, dishes, and inevitably, swords and daggers.

The Neolithic settlements traded with one another—we know this from shells and minerals found in settlements hundreds of miles from their sources. The communities formed alliances of various kinds. But they also made war. The farming revolution was uneven; there always remained nomadic bands envious of the prosperity of their farming neighbors, who would make sudden raids on settlements to snatch up sheep and cattle, stored grains, tools, and weapons. The settlements undoubtedly fought among themselves for access to the best water sources and pastures, to avenge an insult, or simply to establish dominance over a weaker group. For protection, these settlements began to build wooden stockades of poles around their villages. Some groups moved onto islands connected to the mainland by humanmade causeways. The settlements even built "islands" of rafts off lake shores. War was becoming a fact of human life—if it had not already become so long before.

A new stage of human life, and of war, came with the rise of the first civilizations—that is to say, societies based around cities. (*Civilization*

IN ANCIENT TIMES, THE PEOPLES OF THE MIDDLE EAST BEGAN BUILDING WALLED CITIES. IN RESPONSE, THEIR ENEMIES BEGAN DEVISING MEANS OF BREAKING DOWN THESE WALLS. THIS ASSYRIAN BATTERING RAM DATES FROM AT LEAST THE NINTH CENTURY B.C. IT IS A DESIGN THAT WAS THE FORERUNNER OF THE BATTERING RAMS THAT WERE USED UNTIL A BETTER MEANS OF BREACHING WALLS—THE CANNON— WAS DEVELOPED THOUSANDS OF YEARS LATER.

relates to the Latin word for citizen. It is one of the great ironies of history that the more "civilized" people have become, the more deadly their wars have grown.) The first civilizations are generally agreed to have grown up in the Middle East. Here the Sumerians, Assyrians, Babylonians, and later the Egyptians built rich societies based on cities surrounded by fertile farmlands. These peoples developed writing, wheeled vehicles, and calendars. They worked with metals and had taxes, commerce, and complex religions with temples and priesthoods. They were ambitious, and they made war with each other and defended themselves against outside people who envied their prosperity.

Inevitably, they reached out for improved weapons and better tactical schemes. They used bows, spears, swords, shields, and club-headed maces. Metal helmets were produced to protect heads against maces. So the war ax was developed to cut through the helmets. Sometimes these armies used chariots in an attack. They began using the composite bow, made of various combinations of wood, horn, sinews and glue for great strength. These early armies were well organized and fought in disciplined formations. Some of the soldiers wore rudimentary armor composed of small pieces of metal attached to a garment.

There has always been a tendency for warfare to increase by degrees: better weapons are answered by better defensive systems, which in turn gives rise to even more advanced weapons. These early cities constantly strengthened their defenses. Walls seven feet thick (two meters) or even more were built around towns. To combat them, as early as 700 or 600 B.C. battering rams were designed. By 400 B.C. there were siege towers, which could be pushed against fortress walls, allowing attackers to fire into the town. Catapults of various kinds were built to throw stones or burning missiles over town walls.

The point is that by perhaps a thousand years before the birth of Christ, and in many cases several thousand years before that, human beings had created the offensive and defensive weapons and systems that would still be basic to warfare until the gunpowder revolution, which began in about A.D. 1300. The bows, lances, armor, battering rams, and castle walls of the medieval knights we are so familiar with from popular books and movies were only improved versions of the weapons used by the Sumerians thousands of years before. If a soldier who had fought in the armies of the Egyptian Old Kingdom suddenly found himself at the famous Battle of Hastings some 4,000 years later, he would not have found much about it very strange.

To be sure, there were changes. Improved metallurgy allowed lighter steel to be used in place of bronze for swords and armor; new designs improved defensive walls and forts. But the essence of warfare in medieval times was little different from what it had been 5,000 years earlier.

The one major change was the development of cavalry as a powerful fighting force. Horses had long since been trained for pulling and hauling, and by 3500 B.C. the horse-drawn chariot had become a major tool of war in the Middle East. Then, in roughly the fourth century B.C. the stirrup and the horseshoe were invented. The stirrup enabled riders to gain a firmer seat on their mounts, which was essential for a man attempting to drive a lance into an enemy from horseback, while the horseshoe helped to prevent damage to the animals. The use of cavalry had some limitations. In most instances it could only be used extensively in areas where there was plenty of good grazing land and water; and cavalry was not particularly effective in mountains or heavily forested regions. But the advantages of a mass of horsemen charging down on infantry were so obvious that by 400 B.C. cavalry had been added to armies in Greece and elsewhere.

Then, in 378 B.C., as the great Roman Empire was collapsing, an army of Goths attacked the Romans at Adrianople in what is now Turkey. The Goths had originally migrated out of Russia and across central Europe, which was open grassy country, ideal for horses. The Goths had become great riders and understood the use of cavalry. In the middle of the battle at Adrianople, the Gothic chief flung his horsemen against the Romans. They drove the Roman infantry back against the Gothic infantry. The Romans became so tightly packed that they could hardly raise their arms to fight and were soon cut to pieces. The fight at Adrianople was, says one military historian, "the first great victory of heavy cavalry over infantry."

ORIGINATING IN THE ANCIENT CIVILIZATIONS OF THE MIDDLE EAST, MOST ARMOR WAS NOT SOLID PLATES BUT LINKS OF METAL THAT FORMED A LAYER OF PROTECTION FOR THE UPPER PART OF THE BODY. SHOWN HERE IS THE TYPE OF CHAIN MAIL WORN AT THE BATTLE OF HASTINGS IN 1066. THE HELMET IS ROUNDED AT THE TOP TO MAKE SWORD BLOWS GLANCE OFF. THE NOSE GUARD PROVIDES SOME PROTECTION FOR THE FACE, WHILE LEAVING THE EYES FREE.

However, the heyday of cavalry came with the rise of the celebrated armored knight in late medieval times some eight hundred years later. No other warrior has been the subject of so much romantic nonsense as the knight with his castle, heavy sword, lance, and shield emblazoned with his coat of arms. Some of the greatest European literature is built around this romance—Shakespeare's *Henry V* and others of his historic plays, Sir Walter Scott's classic novel *Ivanhoe*, and the stories of Arthur and the Knights of the Round Table, although if Arthur actually existed, he lived long before the age of the knights. Even today movies about knights, tournaments, and personal combat with sword and lance continue to draw audiences. We have no trouble picturing in our minds these knights, their shining armor, and their castles with their turrets, drawbridges, battlements, and waving pennants.

As portrayed in novels, movies, and poems, the courtly knight of medieval times was brave, honest, and bound to perform great feats of arms at the behest of his fair lady. The truth, inevitably, is somewhat different. The medieval knight was part and parcel of what is known as the feudal system. The development of feudalism is complex and much debated. All we need to know is that it was built on a hierarchy of duties and allegiances. During the Middle Ages, for the most part, nations did not really exist in the modern sense of a group of people sharing a piece of ground, a social system, and common loyalties. A king was not so much the ruler of a group of people as the holder of a piece of land or several pieces of land. The English king not only held England, but at times substantial pieces of land elsewhere, particularly in what is now France.

As a consequence, during the heyday of the armored knight, Europe—and other places as well—was a patchwork of small principalities, duchies, cities, and small city-states, which were constantly at odds with each other for power, prestige, even small points of honor. Kings, where they existed, were forever trying to control their squabbling barons, who in their turn sometimes ganged up to replace the king with one of their own. Warfare was constant.

Kings, however, did not have standing armies with which to enforce their laws. In general, they could not afford to keep a large army. Instead they turned over rights to chunks of their land, often the size of American counties, to their main followers in exchange for certain obligations. Among these duties usually was the requirement for the vassal—duke, earl, count—to turn up when called on by the king with a certain number of fighting men, horses, arms, and supplies. These dukes and counts had vassals of their own who received rights to a portion of the land held by the duke in return once again for the obligation to produce so many fighting men when required. In this way kings were frequently able to put together armies of thousands of men and their equipment in order to fight specific wars.

This feudal system was not, however, simply a business transaction. Through the Middle Ages these fighting noblemen adhered to a rigid code that required them to always show the utmost bravery, to fight to the death at the command of their lords, and to never accept an insult or run from a fight, no matter how bad the odds.

A key date in the age of knighthood was the famous year of A.D. 1066, when William the Conqueror won England from King Harold at the Battle of Hastings. Over the previous several hundred years, Norsemen from Scandinavia had been raiding lands to the south, especially England and northwestern Europe. They had taken control of portions of the British Isles, as well as the western part of France we still call Normandy in their honor. William was one of these Normans. He had what he felt was a good claim to the throne of England. In 1066 he sailed for the south coast of England with a substantial force, which included cavalry. The English ruler, Harold, was fighting in the north of his own country. He made a hasty march south and met William's troops at a little place called Hastings. Harold's troops were mainly infantry. They assembled on a rise of ground. William repeatedly sent his cavalry charging at Harold's troops. The massed infantry stood firm, but between charges William ordered his archers to fire into the mass. Gradually the defenders were worn down. The end came when an arrow fired into the air pierced Harold's eye, killing him. A last charge by William's cavalry into the thinning ranks of the now-dispirited defenders broke them down, and they fled. William, with his cavalry and archers, had won England. It was a victory of great historical importance. One outcome was that the old French language spoken by the conquerors combined with the language of Harold's people to produce the English language as we know it. The battle also started England on the way to nationhood, and eventually, by slow, tortuous stages, on the road to democracy. Without the England that grew out of the Battle of Hastings, there would not have been a United States of America.

THIS MEDIEVAL CASTLE STILL STANDS IN CARCASSONNE, FRANCE. THE ROUNDED PROJECTIONS ON THE WALLS ALLOWED DEFENDERS TO SHOOT AT ATTACKERS ATTEMPTING TO CLIMB UP. PARAPETS ALONG THE TOP OF THE WALL GAVE MUCH-NEEDED PROTECTION TO ARCHERS.

William now had to find ways to control his newly won land. He did this by instituting the feudal system, giving his chief followers huge fiefdoms, where they, or William himself, built fortified strong points, which could command the surrounding countryside. These strong points were usually set up at various key places, such as a river crossing or a road junction, and were made largely of wood. They were, in fact, the original castles.

Most of them were arranged on the so-called motte-and-bailey plan. A motte was a ditch surrounding a mound or small hill, either natural or built from the dirt dug out of the motte. (The word *moat* comes from *motte*.) A wooden stockade was built inside the motte, around the mound. Inside the stockade there was erected a fortified house of wood, called the donjon, from which we get our word *dungeon*. The lord, his family, and retainers lived in the donjon.

Outside the motte a second stockade was built, and outside that a second motte. The protected area between the two stockades was called the bailey. In times of danger, cattle, sheep, and other livestock from the surrounding farms were driven into the bailey. This way the livestock was not only protected, but could serve as food if the castle was besieged. Such castles were always built with a good water source; with livestock and water they were often able to hold out against a siege for weeks, if not months.

These wooden castles, however, were vulnerable to attack by battering rams, catapults, and especially fire, which could be started by flaming arrows shot into the walls. By the end of the eleventh century, not long after William's conquest of England in 1066, the lords began to build their castles out of stone. A popular new arrangement was the shell-keep, a roughly circular high stone wall that surrounded an area perhaps a hundred feet (thirty meters) across. A keep, or tower, was set into the wall, usually at a defensible place, such as where the ground below happened to be steep. The walls might be as much as eighty feet (twenty-four meters) high, the height of a tall tree. Frequently there was a second wall around the whole to create a bailey, and possibly additional baileys as well. Entrance was via drawbridges over the mottes, and the gate through the walls could be closed with thick wooden doors. The lord, his family, and retainers lived in the keep, which had few windows and was lighted mainly by arrow slits in the walls. Life inside a castle keep was very rough. Light was provided by candles and burning rushes or reeds; heat came from fireplaces, and in winter the stone floors and walls were inevitably cold. There was very little privacy: even the lord might not have a bedroom of his own, but would share a room with his family and retainers. Most of the people in the castle slept on bedding in a room with many others.

At the time of William I, knights were not clothed in the glistening armor we know from movies and books. They wore instead thigh-length chain mail, made of hundreds of tiny metal ringlets linked together and shaped overall like a dress. This chain mail was surprisingly effective against sword thrusts. The knights wore conical helmets as well, usually with a noseguard. William's infantry carried spears and in some cases huge battle-axes, which they swung with two hands to cut through chain mail or even metal helmets.

The mounted knights fought with swords and lances, but by the time of the Battle of Hastings a new weapon was beginning to be widely used: the crossbow. The bow was mounted horizontally on a stock somewhat like a modern gunstock. The bow itself was a composite of wood, horn, glue, and leather and was so stiff that it couldn't be drawn by hand. Some were drawn by crank-handled ratchets, some by levers or other means. In time, crossbows of wood, leather, and horn were replaced

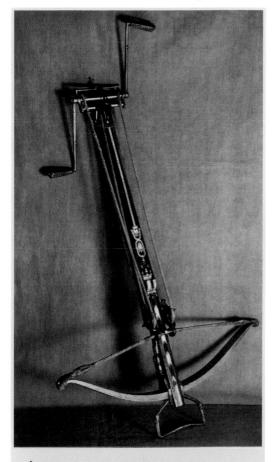

A VARIETY OF SYSTEMS AND TECHNIQUES WAS USED TO DRAW BACK THE STRINGS OF CROSSBOWS. IN THIS EXAMPLE, THE BOW IS DRAWN BY A SYSTEM OF PULLEYS AND CRANKS. THE BOLT WAS THEN SHOT WITH A FORCE GREAT ENOUGH TO PENETRATE ARMOR. HOWEVER, IN BATTLE, CROSSBOWS WERE SLOWER TO USE THAN THE LONGBOW.

AS ATTACKERS AND DEFENDERS BECAME MORE AGGRESSIVE IN THEIR ATTEMPTS TO OVERPOWER EACH OTHER, ARMOR BECAME MORE AND MORE ELABORATE. EVENTUALLY THE ENTIRE BODY, INCLUDING THE FINGERS, WAS COVERED IN STEEL PLATE. NOTE THE POINTED VISOR, WHICH IS DESIGNED SO THAT ARROWS OR LANCES WILL BE DIRECTED AWAY TO THE SIDES OF THE HELMET AND AWAY FROM THE FACE.

by metal ones. They shot short "bolts" of metal, usually equipped with metal "feathers" at the tail for stability in flight, and frequently were headed by several points. Crossbows were slow to load and shoot, but they could penetrate chain mail, even solid steel. So deadly was the crossbow that the pope outlawed it for use against Christians, although nobody paid any attention to the edict.

As weapons became more deadly, knights began wearing the famous solid steel armor that now is displayed in museums, starting with breastplates and gradually adding coverings for hands, arms, legs, and feet. By the end of the medieval period, most knights were entirely sheathed in steel. Helmets and breastplates were made pointed or convex so arrows would slide off them. This armor was so heavy that a knight needed the help of a squire or two to mount his horse. If he were knocked off he might have difficulty getting to his feet, especially if he had been wounded. After some battles, enemy infantry went among the fallen knights killing them with daggers shoved through helmet slits or even slicing them open like lobsters with battle-axes. Horses, too, were outfitted with armor.

Clashes between mounted knights were often disorganized, and some knights believed that behaving strategically was unchivalrous—a little unfair, even cowardly. Often the knights, seeking personal glory in battle, ignored the commands of their leaders. After the initial charge with lances, battles usually broke into the melee, in which each knight took on one of the enemy in single combat. Despite the uproar and clanking of arms and armor, relatively few knights were actually killed in battle. It was far better to disable your enemy, capture him, and hold him for ransom. Kings generally led their knights into battle, and these rulers made important prizes when captured, for they would bring "a king's ransom," which might be enough to impoverish a whole nation. The celebrated Richard the Lion-Hearted of England was captured and held for a ransom of 3 million pounds, billions of dollars in today's money. According to legend, Richard's good friend Blondel wandered around Europe trying to discover where Richard was held. He sang Richard's favorite song under castle walls. When Richard heard Blondel he began to sing along. He was soon ransomed.

In fact, set battles, such as the Battle of Hastings, were relatively rare. As odd as it may seem, hostile armies of knights at times had trouble finding each other, however determined they were to have a fight. Maps in those days were poor or nonexistent. Much of the warfare of the time consisted of armies, even small bands of knights, making raids in enemy territory and pillaging unfortunate peasants.

For much of this time, infantry was of little use. Most infantrymen were peasants called up for battle and equipped with whatever they had at hand, which were often farm tools such as implements for chopping branches. The infantry was easily ridden down by armored knights.

So, most medieval warfare involved attacking or defending castles. From the eleventh to the fifteenth centuries, constant attempts were made to improve fortifications, which were inevitably answered by new means of attack. Attackers brought into play huge stone-throwing devices, called trebuchets, ballistas, and onagers, which employed different principles. Attackers also used the battering ram—a long, heavy log usually with a metal head, which hung from the roof of a portable shed. The shed was carried, or wheeled, up to the castle wall, and the men inside would slam the hanging log against the walls. The heavy leather roof of the shed protected the men swinging the ram from arrows or boiling water poured down from above.

Mining was another method for bringing down a wall. Attackers would start tunneling toward the castle from some hidden point and dig until they were under the wall. Here they would hollow out a large cave, putting in heavy timbers to support the dirt roof of the cave, on which the wall above stood. They would then set the timbers on fire. When the timbers burned through, the dirt roof would collapse, bringing down the wall above. Attackers would then rush into the gap.

Sometimes attackers would attempt a direct assault. They would charge the castle, fling ladders against the wall, and attempt to climb over. Another method was to wheel a siege tower up against the castle wall. Attacking troops would climb up inside the tower to the top, where they could shoot arrows down into the castle. These direct attacks, however, were rarely successful: defenders usually were able to push the ladders back or disable attackers as their heads came into view.

Inevitably castle defenses were improved. Walls were made thicker and thicker; some were twenty or thirty feet (six or nine meters) thick. Defenders learned how to defeat miners, by tunneling from inside the castle into the attackers' tunnel and fighting them there. Perhaps most important, various types of projections were added to castle walls, which allowed defenders to shoot back toward attackers at the walls. Among these was a kind of platform of stone or wood with holes in it allowing defenders to shoot or pour boiling water on attackers at the walls. Also important were towers attached to the outside of the castle walls, from which defenders could shoot arrows toward or away from their own walls.

Thus it went, back and forth, with defenders and attackers each trying to get an edge. In fact, a stalemate had been reached. A well-planned castle could only be taken with great difficulty. The only sensible thing was to besiege the castle and starve the defenders out. If the castle was well provisioned and had a good supply of water, defenders could hold out for months, and many did. Meanwhile the attacking king or baron was forced to buy supplies for his troops and in some cases pay them; a siege was expensive and in the end attackers often gave up or negotiated terms with the defenders.

In the open field the armored knights were invincible, except against another force of knights, and through the twelfth and thirteenth centuries knights reigned supreme. But then, in the early 1300s, changes started to occur that would bring an end to the glorious days of the armored knight and his castle.

The first of these changes was a new tactical system. In the early 1300s European armies developed a scheme of fighting with pikes (heavy spears), which would prove effective against mounted knights. The Swiss were particularly important in working out this tactic and for a while could not be beaten. The pike involved was eighteen feet (five meters) long and was fitted with a ten-inch (twenty-five-centimeter) steel point. Swiss pikemen fought in close ranks, and because their weapons were so long, the pikes of the first four ranks stuck out beyond the mass of troops to form a bristling wall of steel points. If the pikemen held firm, they could skewer charging horses and knights, driving their pikes through joints in the armor. For some 200 years, Swiss pikemen rarely lost a battle. The Swiss were typically not pressed into service and fought from choice. They were thus well motivated.

A second critically important new weapon was the longbow. It was, in fact, probably the most deadly weapon created by humans until the advent of the repeating rifle during the American Civil War. It was probably developed by the Welsh, although that is not certain. In any case, Edward I of England, a brilliant commander, saw its value and began to use longbowmen as a regular part of his armies.

The English longbow was about 6 feet 4 inches (193 cm) high. It was usually made of yew, a tough wood, although other kinds of wood were also used. It had a draw weight, or "pull," of about 100 pounds, and would send the 37-inch (94-cm) "cloth-yard shaft," or arrow, with such power that it could kill at 250 yards (230 m), about twice the distance from home plate to deep centerfield in most major-league baseball parks. A trained longbowman could fire as many as twenty arrows per minute, although the usual rate in the heat of battle was considerably lower. So powerful was the longbow, that in one case on record a cloth-yard shaft went through a mounted knight's leg, through his horse, and through the knight's other leg, effectively pinning him to the horse. Not until the Civil War could any weapon fire as rapidly and with such accuracy as the longbow in skilled hands.

Edward I used the longbow in his conquest of the Welsh, but it became famous in the Hundred Years' War between England and France, especially in a series of celebrated English victories at Crécy (1346), Poitiers (1356), and Agincourt (1415). Although the battle of Agincourt, made famous by Shakespeare in his play *Henry V,* is the most celebrated of these, Crécy was where the longbow first gained its renown.

The English king of the time, Edward III, felt he had a claim to the throne of France. To enforce that claim, he brought a force of about 12,000 troops to France and, after some maneuvering, met the French just outside the little village of Crécy-en-Ponthieu. Edward stationed his men along a broad slope: the armored knights on foot in the center, the longbowmen on the flanks.

The French arrived at the battlefield at the end of the day. They far outnumbered the English, but they were facing into the setting sun. Furthermore, the French king did not have good control of his forces. He preferred to wait and fight the next day, which would allow him time to plan his attack and rest his troops. However, some of his subordinates, sure of victory against the outnumbered English and full of typical knightly bravado, decided to charge. They did so in considerable confusion. The English bowmen let loose. They knocked down virtually every French knight in the charge. A second wave attacked over the dead and dying knights. This too was cut down. Still, the lesson was not learned. In all, the French made perhaps fifteen suicidal charges, trying to get at the English knights. Occasionally a few made contact with the English, but most of them fell to the cloth-yard shafts before they reached the English ranks. At one point the nearly blind, aged king of Bohemia, an ally of the French king, beset by an excess of chivalry, insisted that some courtiers lead him toward the English. They did, and all were killed. In the morning the field before the English was heaped with the remains of thousands of knights, many of them still in their polished armor. Although nobody had realized it yet, the day of the armored knight was over.

The castle, which could not be taken by the longbow, still reigned. But a weapon was coming that would end its day too: gunpowder.

Gunpowder Changes the Ways of War

Considering the profound effect gunpowder has had on human life—and human death—it is startling that we know so little about its invention. We do not know who invented it, where, or when. Long before true gunpowder, the Byzantine armies of eastern Europe employed something known as Greek fire, which may have existed earlier. This was a compound of various substances including sulfur, pitch, quicklime, natural petroleum, which seeped out of the ground, and naphtha, a fluid distilled from the petroleum. The mixture was highly flammable and hard to extinguish with water. Arrows dipped in Greek fire could be ignited and shot into the enemy. However, it was mainly used by the Byzantines in ship battles, either blown from a large tube by pumps, or heaved onto an enemy ship by a catapult. Greek fire could be effective, but it never became a major instrument of war.

Some historians consider Greek fire a precursor to gunpowder. There is, however, a major distinction between them: gunpowder is an explosive, and Greek fire is not. An explosive is simply a compound that burns with extreme rapidity. (Some modern explosives, such as those used in nuclear weapons, work according to different principles.) As in any process of combustion, heat, light, and gas are given off. In particular the gas expands in a fraction of a second and presses powerfully on whatever is around it,

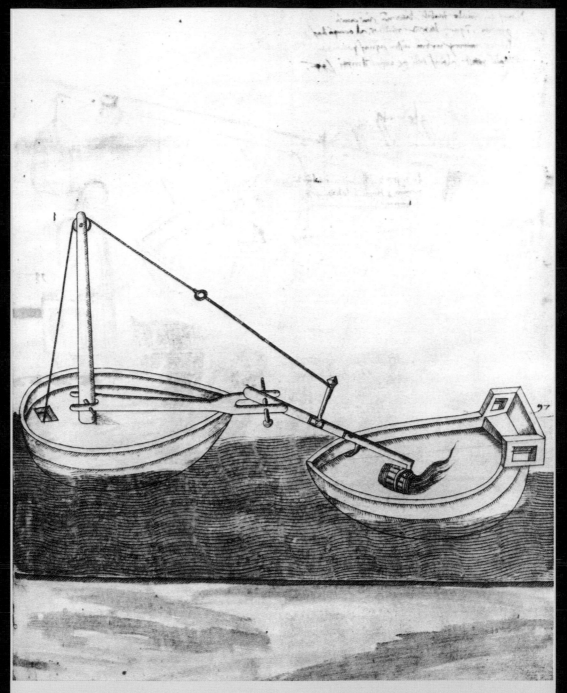

Burning enemy ships was a strategy dating back to Greece's Golden Age, or about 500 B.C., and was still in use a thousand years later. In the fifteenth century A.D., an Italian designed this device for setting opponents' ships on fire.

whether it is the paper on a firecracker or the bullet in a gun barrel. In the process the surrounding air is disturbed, creating a confused, but usually very loud, sound. Depending on the type of explosive, there may also be a flash of light and a cloud of smoke, as was the case with early gunpowders.

It may seem curious to today's readers, but before the invention of gunpowder, few human beings had ever heard an explosion, except a very rare natural one, as in a volcano or when a forest fire by chance ignited a pocket of natural gas. The closest thing to an explosion that most people had heard was thunder. We must keep this in mind when we see how disturbed soldiers were when they were first exposed to gunfire.

In the mid-1200s an English genius named Roger Bacon published a recipe for the substance we know as gunpowder. Bacon was troubled by the grave dangers he saw in this alarming new material, so he was cagey about it. He said, in any case, that if it was enclosed in a small parcel and ignited, it made a tremendous and thoroughly frightening noise. He noted that children sometimes amused themselves by setting off what we would today call firecrackers.

What was this substance? It was really very simple—a combination of charcoal, sulfur, and saltpeter. Charcoal was made by the controlled burning of wood and had been used to make fires from ancient times. Sulfur was not natural everywhere, but was nonetheless fairly common and easy to obtain. Saltpeter was a nitrate created mainly by the action of bacteria on nitrogenous material, especially animal waste, found in medieval barnyards everywhere. Saltpeter was the most complicated of these ingredients to manufacture, but even so it was not difficult to do. The barnyard waste was allowed to sit for as much as a year while acted on by bacteria. Then the saltpeter was purified out in various ways. At first, most saltpeter was calcium nitrate, but in time other nitrates came into use. Once the ingredients were gathered, they were pounded together in a mortar.

Gunpowder was made from materials that were readily available in most places, usually in substantial quantities. The manufacturing process took some care—in the early days a good many gunpowder mills blew up and were therefore usually placed well away from towns and villages. Despite the danger, it was not difficult to learn how to make, and as a consequence, it was always in good supply.

Because of his early writings, for some time many people believed that Roger Bacon had actually invented gunpowder. However, there is now strong evidence that gunpowder was invented by the Chinese. When and where we do not know, but by A.D. 1000 the Chinese were using small bombs, or grenades, in warfare. They also developed a "fire lance," which was a gunpowder rocket to which a gunpowder bomb was attached. However, none of these gunpowder weapons became important tools of war for the Chinese: their greatest effect seems to have been the loud bang they made, which struck awe into the hearts of enemy troops.

Whether the Chinese went on to invent the cannon is hard to determine. One great authority on Chinese science, Joseph Needham, says that they did. However, the evidence is scanty. Whatever the case, it is certain that the Chinese did not go on to develop gunpowder weapons or to use them extensively in warfare until later.

For better or worse, gunpowder weapons were developed in Europe. Before roughly A.D. 1100 Europe was something of an intellectual backwater: the Chinese and the Muslim nations, and possibly others, were well ahead of the Europeans in science and technology. Then, beginning in about the twelfth century, Europeans began to speed up their technological development. It was a trend of immense importance, for in Europe technology spiraled upward at an ever-increasing pace, and by the nineteenth century, Europeans were able to dominate much of the rest of the world. That is no longer the case, but it is true that "the West," including Europe and its descendants, such as the United States, continue to have a powerful influence on the rest of the world. This trend began with the technological burst of the late medieval period.

The development of gunpowder weapons, and all that grew out of it, began sometime around the year A.D. 1300. Once again, exactly where and when it happened we do not know. Cannons are mentioned in an Italian document of 1326. In the same year there appeared a manuscript by Walter de Milemete, now in Christ Church, Oxford, England, containing a picture

ALTHOUGH IT IS DIFFICULT TO JUDGE ITS SIZE IN THIS MEDIEVAL PAINTING, IN WHICH PERSPECTIVE AND PROPORTION ARE SLIGHTLY SKEWED, THE CANNONS OF THE DAY WERE TYPICALLY SMALL. THEY WERE USED PRIMARILY TO ASSAULT CASTLE WALLS. LONGBOWS AND CROSSBOWS WERE STILL THE WEAPONS OF CHOICE.

that clearly shows a cannon. There is another picture of a cannon in the so-called Holkham Hall manuscript of about the same time, although the date of the picture is not certain. A manuscript of 1339 in Guildhall in London mentions "gonnes" and powder. All of this evidence makes it clear that by the early 1300s cannons were known and in use in western Europe.

These early cannons were relatively small. The one in the Milemete illustration appears to be about three or four feet (one meter) long, although it is unwise to make judgments about the size of things in medieval paintings, which were usually not drawn to scale. The Milemete cannon is pear shaped, looking something like a large vase laid on its side. It was curved at the back end probably because the cannon walls there were made thicker, as this area took the brunt of the explosion. Its projectile was often an arrow with a four-sided head, probably a standard crossbow bolt. Arrow projectiles remained in use for some time, but in general these early cannons shot heavy, round stones, like the ones soldiers had fired at them from catapults.

These early cannons were made of bronze or, in a few cases, copper. Many of them were cast by bell makers, who were experienced in making large pieces. By about 1370 iron was being used more widely. Iron was more difficult to cast than bronze, so iron cannons were usually made of iron bars laid around a frame. The iron bars were bound together by iron hoops, as in a barrel, and then were heated to fuse the metal parts.

The first cannons were muzzle loaders—that is, the powder and ball were inserted from the front end of the gun. However, certainly by 1400 and probably earlier, breechloaders, which were charged from the rear of the gun, were being made. The whole question of muzzle loading versus breech loading would bedevil gunners for centuries. Breech loading was safer and more convenient than muzzle loading. But there was one paramount disadvantage to the breechloader. When the gun was loaded, the breech had to be closed with a strong, tight-fitting cover of some kind in order to prevent the explosive gas from escaping (and thus lessening the force needed to propel the bullet or cannon ball) or actually blowing off the breech cover. Not until the late nineteenth century, when improved machinery for working metal was devised, was the problem really solved. Nonetheless breechloaders continued in use, although muzzle loaders were more common.

Precisely when cannons were first installed on ships is not known. Because people traveled so often by water, cannons were being carried onto ships quite early in their development. The idea of firing a cannon from a ship, either at another ship or at a walled port city, was an obvious one, and by the fifteenth century rudimentary "battleships" equipped with cannons were in use. However, the real development of shipboard cannons came in the sixteenth century, when European explorers, traders, and conquistadors were traveling around the world to trade for, or simply seize, vast quantities of valuable goods, including gold and silver. These treasure ships were natural prey for pirates and the fleets of rival nations, so ships began to carry increasing numbers of cannons, along with hand-held guns for both attack and defense.

The key point in all of this is that the Europeans were quick to see the possibilities of gunpowder weapons. Edward III of England is reported to have used cannons in his campaigns to subdue Scotland in 1327, although that is not certain. He definitely took guns to France for the Battle of Crécy in 1346—probably three small cannons like the ones pictured in the Milemete painting. It was the longbow, not cannons, that made the difference in the fight, but cannons fired into a body of French archers caused them to flee, as much from the noise and smoke as from the balls landing among them.

It was soon understood that the cannon's greatest value came in demolishing the walls of towns, cities, and castles. A stone cannonball driven by gunpowder hit a lot harder than one flung from a catapult. It was also clear that the bigger the ball, the harder it hit. Cannons began to grow in size. By the 1370s there were cannons 21 inches (53 cm) in diameter, a good size compared even with modern guns. Such a weapon could fire a stone ball weighing 450 pounds (200 kg). In 1453 the Turks had a huge bronze cannon with a caliber—inside diameter—of 3 feet (1 meter), which fired a ball weighing more than 600 pounds (270 kg) a mile and a half (2.4 km).

THE BATTLE OF SLUYS, IN WHICH THE ENGLISH BEAT THE FRENCH IN JUNE 1340, WAS ONE OF THE LARGEST BATTLES OF ITS TIME. ALTHOUGH CANNONS WERE THEN IN USE, THEY WERE PROBABLY NOT EMPLOYED AT SLUYS. HOWEVER, SHIPS LIKE THE ONES SHOWN HERE WERE EVENTUALLY FITTED WITH CANNONS FOR SEA BATTLES AND TO ATTACK PORTS, AS PORTS WERE MORE FREQUENTLY UNDER SIEGE.

THE FAMOUS CZAR'S CANNON, STILL A TOURIST ATTRACTION IN RUSSIA, COMES FROM A LATER PERIOD, BUT IS SOME INDICATION OF THE SIZE CANNONS ACHIEVED WHEN THEY WERE BEING USED PRIMARILY TO KNOCK DOWN THE WALLS OF FORTIFICATIONS.

Some of these cannons were given pet names, often after women. The French had one firing a 500-pound (227-kg) ball they called Garite, which was short for Margarite.

But while such huge guns hit hard, they were very difficult to transport, especially in a time when roads, if they existed, were mostly muddy cart tracks, and streams were unbridged. Most cannons had bores—interior diameters—of 1 to 2 feet (0.3 m to 0.6 m) and were 10 to 15 feet (3 to 4.6 m) in length. Such guns were not easy to transport either, but they could be moved more easily than monsters like Garite. In fact, a lot of cannons were meant to be stationary. By the later 1300s in England, France, Germany, and elsewhere, many towns were buying cannons to be set in town walls for defense: in 1386 the city of Calais, on the English Channel, ordered sixty of them.

Over the course of the 1300s, as the longbow was bringing an inglorious end to the dominance of the armored knight, so gunpowder weapons were ending the reign of the castle. A key battle came in 1415 when Henry V landed in France—yet one more English king determined to assert rights to French lands. Henry eventually won the Battle of Agincourt, but in preparation for it, he laid siege to the French port city of Harfleur. The city was enclosed by thick walls and was well defended. Henry, however, had brought with him from England some very large cannons, with names such as The King's Daughter and London. For twenty-seven days Henry's cannons banged away at a portion of a Harfleur wall around a gate, reducing it to rubble. The wooden parts of the gate were then set on fire by an incendiary shell. Henry's troops charged into the gap, and Harfleur quickly surrendered. According to one military authority, "When Henry V's artillery battered down the walls of Harfleur in 1415 the era of impregnable fortifications passed." With the demise of the knight and the castle, the offense began to catch up with the defense. Not until the nineteenth century would the defense again have the advantage.

But as always, who lives by the sword dies by the sword. As a consequence of Henry's famous victory at Agincourt and other battles, he was able to claim all of Normandy, the northwestern area of France, for himself. After his death, however, another famous fighter, Joan of Arc, roused the French to fight back. At that time the French had "the first great artilleryman," Jean Bureau. In a single year, from 1449 to 1450, Bureau and his cannons took by siege sixty English strong points in Normandy—a rate of about five per month. Never again would the English be a force in France.

By the time the French were knocking down the English castles in Normandy, European gunners had had a hundred years of experience with gunpowder and were well aware of its drawbacks. One recurring problem was its tendency to get damp in wet weather. Even if the powder was not actually wet, it might still absorb moisture from the air on rainy days, making it useless until it was dry again. This original "serpentine" powder was ground very fine so as to make it burn more rapidly. Sometime before 1420 it was discovered that if the powder was dampened, formed into small loaves, or dumplings, and was allowed to dry, it absorbed less moisture, the idea being that powder lumped together this way exposed less total surface to the air than when it was in powder form. To be used, it had to be once again broken into bits, or "crumbed," as the term came to be. In time it was discovered that gunpowder burned faster when it was crumbed to a size somewhere between a grain of coarse salt and a grain of rice. These early gunners had started out looking for a way to keep their powder dry, but had come up with a significantly more powerful form of gunpowder.

This new, more potent crumbed or "corned" powder had important consequences. One was that since it was able to drive a denser ball, there was an increasing tendency to replace stone balls with cast-iron ones. But stone cannonballs had the advantage of splintering when they hit a wall and showering sharp fragments among the defenders. On the other hand, the heavier cast-iron balls were invaluable in knocking down fortresses.

Another advantage of corned powder was that because the balls now hit with more power, it was possible to use smaller ones, driven by less powder. This in turn meant that guns could be smaller, with somewhat thinner walls—all great advantages in manufacturing.

Corned powder was particularly advantageous for handheld guns. Soldiers had realized quite early that a small cannon that could be carried around and fired by one man might be useful against enemy troops. By 1350 various types of handheld guns were being devised. The first of these were quite small and simple, little more than barrels less than a foot (0.3 m) long attached to wooden poles, or hafts. Like cannons, they had a touchhole on the top through which the gun was fired. These early handheld guns were extremely awkward to use. In order to fire one, the gunner had to pick up a hot coal or hot piece of metal with a pair of tongs and then apply it to the touchhole. He could hardly aim while going through this procedure. Sometimes the gun barrel was propped up on a stick or supported by another soldier, but neither system helped much with aiming.

Furthermore, the gunner apparently held the pole to which the barrel was attached clamped under an arm and had to absorb the recoil with his arms. It was clearly a poor system, and over the next hundred years improvements were made. For one thing, barrels were made longer to increase accuracy. For another, curved stocks were worked out, which allowed the gunner to hold the stock against his chest to better aim and absorb the recoil. In time the shoulder stock, still in use, was devised.

Most important, step-by-step changes were made in the method of firing. Probably before 1400 the touchhole was moved down to the side of the barrel. Right under it was set a small "pan" an inch or two (2.5 or 5 cm) in length. To fire the weapon a small amount of powder was poured into the pan. When this priming powder exploded it ignited the powder inside the barrel. With this system the gunner was better able to maintain control of his weapon while firing it.

But it was far from a perfect system. The key development came, probably shortly after 1400, with the invention of a device that was attached to the gun itself. In essence this was a clamp holding a slow-burning wick or match that could be swiveled by a lever into the pan when it was time to fire. With this device the shooter could continue to keep his eye on the target while he swiveled the match into the pan.

Nonetheless, this device still left the gunner with only one hand free to steady the weapon while he swiveled the match into the priming pan. Something better was needed, and not long after 1450 the famous matchlock was developed. In this design a set of linked levers pushed the clamp holding the wick into the pan. The clamp had a spring attached, which pushed it back out of the pan. In this system the gunner could use both his left hand and the heel of his right hand to steady the gun while he pulled a lever that dropped the match into the pan. The matchlock would be the standard army weapon for 200 years.

Two refinements were soon added. A spring was now set to snap the match into the powder, which meant that the clamp holding the match had to be held back by a catch until it was time to fire. When the lever was pulled, the catch was released and the clamp was snapped forward. The gun now had a real trigger, but not everybody was happy with this system, as sometimes the match was propelled downward so rapidly it went out. And because the catch was released by only a small pressure on the trigger, it often went off by mistake, with unfortunate results. For safety purposes yet another device was added, a cover for the pan, which was removed by the action of the firing mechanism. But the snapping matchlock did not become popular: the less complicated version remained the standard army and hunting weapon for some time to come.

At the same time, bullets were becoming standardized. In the early days gunners had experimented with many shapes and materials. Gradually the ball became the preferred shape and lead the material of choice. Lead was dense enough to hit with power, but it had a low melting point and could be manufactured by soldiers in the field and by farmers at home. It was also much cheaper than many other types of metal.

By 1500 the first cartridges were being used. These were not the modern cartridges we are familiar with, which have a bullet and powder contained in a metal shell. Instead they were devised to make loading easier. Enough powder for one shot was placed inside a small bag of linen or vellum (a type of treated animal skin). To load, the gunner ripped open the bag with his teeth, poured the powder in, dropped the ball in afterward, and rammed home the empty bag which acted as a wad holding everything tight. With these prepared cartridges, loading was significantly speeded up, and less powder was spilled.

The early matchlocks came in a variety of shapes and sizes. The term *arquebus* was quite common and was usually applied to lighter guns. *Musket* meant a heavier gun that originally had to be supported by a forked rest under the barrel. Other terms were used as well, but whatever the term, matchlocks were slow. The shooter had to remove the match for safety, turn the gun muzzle up, load it, push everything together with the ramrod, replace the match, aim, and fire. For a long time the bow, especially the longbow, actually was a better weapon than the gun. It was just as accurate, carried a considerable distance, and could be fired much more rapidly than a matchlock.

But for warfare the gun had certain advantages. For one, learning how to use it did not take years of practice, as did the longbow. Army recruits could be taught how to use a matchlock in weeks, if not days—a fact that would have important consequences, as we will shortly see. For another, these early guns with their relatively large balls hit with a tremendous impact. A ball would tear up flesh, break bones, and usually knock the victim down. A wound even to a nonvital organ could incapacitate a man and would surely make him wish he were someplace else.

Wars were critically important matters, both to the rulers who started them and the men who actually fought them. Everybody was looking for faster, more accurate, safer weapons, and soon another step forward was taken. The new device, simple in theory, turned out to be more complicated in practice. It consisted of a small wheel of steel into which little notches had been cut and a piece of iron pyrite, a yellow mineral. When the notched wheel was spun against the pyrite, a shower of sparks was given off. If directed into a pan filled with gunpowder, the sparks would ignite the powder. It worked, in fact, very much like a modern cigarette lighter.

But there were complications. The wheel was spun by a chain going around its axle, which in turn was pulled by a tightly wound spring. There had to be a cocking mechanism to hold the wheel in place after it was wound up, a trigger, and yet another mechanism to slide the pan cover away when the wheel started to let off sparks. Some models included various safety devices, which added to the complexity. This style of firearm was quite expensive because building the mechanism required skilled workers, often clock makers, who were used to working with wheels and springs. But the wheel lock, as it was called, had a tremendous advantage: once it was loaded and cocked, it could be carried around indefinitely and fired at a moment's notice.

When the wheel lock was invented is not known for certain. It was probably very early in the 1500s, possibly in northern Italy or southern Germany, where many of the early examples that we have today were

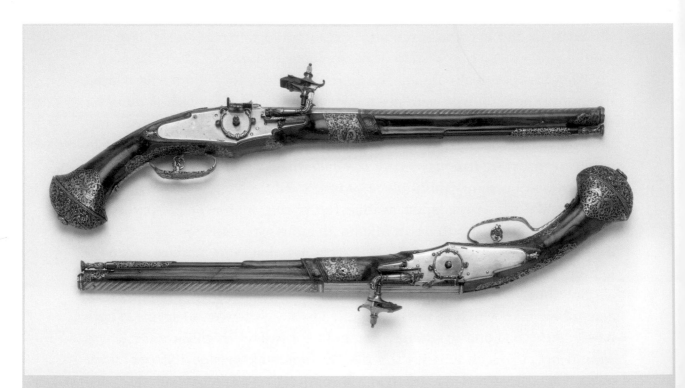

WHEEL-LOCK PISTOLS WERE EXPENSIVE TO MAKE, BECAUSE OF THEIR INTRICATE MECHANISMS. THEY WERE ALSO DANGER-OUS, SOMETIMES DISCHARGING ACCIDENTALLY. HOWEVER, THEY COULD BE LOADED AND COCKED IN ADVANCE AND READY TO FIRE AT A MOMENT'S NOTICE, WHICH MADE THEM AN IDEAL CHOICE FOR BOTH CRIMINALS AND FEARFUL TOWNSPEOPLE. CAVALRY OFFICERS, WHO NEEDED ONE HAND FREE WITH WHICH TO MANAGE THEIR HORSES, ALSO FAVORED THE WEAPONS.

made. The wheel lock was immediately taken up by criminals, who had previously used daggers and swords. As early as 1517, an Austrian ruler banned the making of wheel locks, in part because they were used increasingly in murders, in part because they often went off accidentally. By the 1520s many Italian cities had similar rules. Enforcing the wheel-lock bans was difficult, though, because wheel-lock pistols could be hidden under coats and jackets.

Cavalry officers, too, took up the wheel lock, because it left one hand free to hold a horse's reins. The pistol, both handy and concealable, rose in popularity, and another step toward modern firearms had been taken.

But for armies the matchlock continued to be the preferred weapon; it was simply too expensive for a ruler to equip a large army with wheel locks. But more progress was on the way. In a short time a variety of simpler versions of the wheel lock appeared, called snapping locks. Remember that the old snapping matchlock never came into favor because the force of the snap often extinguished the match. With the wheel lock that problem no longer existed. In a snapping lock, a piece of flint was held by a jaw clamp set onto a cock of steel that could swivel forward so the flint scraped along the surface of a piece of steel set above the priming pan. As in the wheel lock, the scraping of steel and flint gave off a shower of sparks. The cock was held back—or "cocked"—by a catch, and was snapped forward by a heavy spring when the trigger was pulled.

Yet again we are not sure precisely when the first snapping weapon was made; it was probably not long after the introduction of the wheel lock. Over the next century many types of guns utilizing the snapping principle were made—snaphaunces, miquelets, dog locks, and more. These weapons were more complex than the old matchlocks, but they were simpler and cheaper to make than wheel locks. Rulers were still reluctant to outfit their armies with them, but inevitably through the 1500s they grew in popularity. They were carried to the New World by the English colonists of Jamestown and Plymouth, where they were critically important in hunting the wild turkeys, deer, and other game that kept the early colonists alive.

Then, sometime after 1610, a French craftsman named Marin Le

WHEN THE TRIGGER OF THE FLINTLOCK WAS PULLED BACK, THE CLAMP HOLDING THE PIECE OF FLINT SNAPPED FORWARD AS THE STEEL MOVED BACK INTO THE POSITION WHERE IT WOULD BE STRUCK. SPARKS FLEW INTO THE PAN, FIRING THE POWDER.

Bourgeoys from the village of Lisieux in Normandy created an improved snapping gun: the famous flintlock. Le Bourgeoys introduced a small technical change in the firing mechanism that made the gun less likely to go off accidentally and made it more reliable in general. The flintlock soon became the most popular weapon, and by 1700 it was being used in most major European armies.

Flintlocks were made in a great variety of sizes and weights. For Americans, two of the best-known types were the "Brown Bess," as the standard British army weapon was known, and the Charleville, named for an important French arms center. The French and Indian War, the American Revolution, and the War of 1812 were mainly fought with these flintlocks.

The development of these weapons, from the matchlock to the flint-lock, changed the nature of war in Europe and eventually in the rest of the world. Now massed infantry could gun down charging cavalry before the riders could get near enough to the foot soldiers to kill them or ride them down. Cavalrymen could, of course, carry guns, but it was difficult to shoot from horseback, particularly at full charge. The cavalryman was only really effective at close quarters where he could use a sword or lance. And up against reliable guns, he was likely to be dead before he got that close. The dominance of the cavalry was over, although mounted troops would continue to be used for special purposes for some time to come.

It was now clear that victory depended on using massive firepower. Matchlocks and flintlocks could fire only a single shot and took time to re-load. This meant that there had to be enough soldiers so that some were firing while others reloaded. Armies began to grow, as did the death toll.

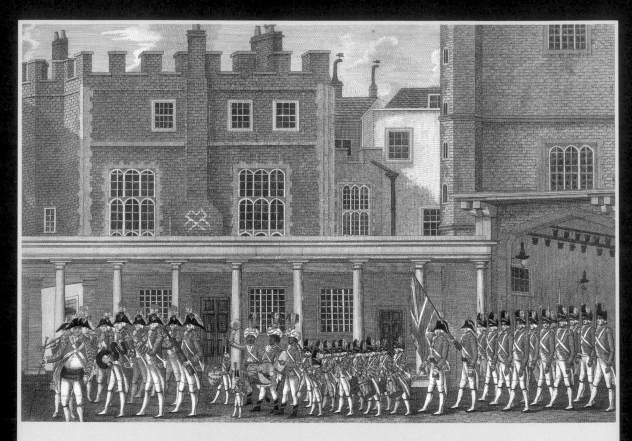

BEFORE THE SEVENTEENTH CENTURY, ARMIES HAD BEEN MADE UP OF FARMERS AND WHOEVER ELSE WAS AVAILABLE. RECRUITS MIGHT SERVE FOR THE LENGTH OF A BRIEF WAR OR EVEN A BATTLE, USING WHATEVER ARMS THEY HAD ON HAND. BY THE SEVENTEENTH CENTURY, ARMIES WERE MOSTLY COMPOSED OF PROFESSIONAL FIGHTERS. AS THIS EIGHTEENTH-CENTURY PARADE OF ENGLISH SOLDIERS REVEALS, TROOPS WERE AT THAT TIME WEARING STANDARD UNIFORMS, USING STANDARD WEAPONS, AND WERE THOROUGHLY DRILLED AND TRAINED.

THREE

The Rise of the Professional Army

In writing about battles, war historians are inclined to talk about one general "smashing the center" of the enemy line, or "turning the enemy's flank with his reserves," and so on. This style of writing often makes it appear that war is like a football game, or even a chess match, with one commander "countering" the other's moves by shifting his forces this way or that, as if he were advancing his pawns and rooks.

We must keep in mind that "turning the enemy's flank" and similar maneuvers are accompanied by fearsome and bloody slaughter with men's bellies sliced open, their legs ripped off, and their heads split in half. Nobody who has ever seen the field after a battle will forget it: hundreds perhaps thousands of corpses lying grotesquely twisted, arms, legs, and heads missing, strips of torn and bloody flesh, dying men begging hoarsely for help or simply moaning half-conscious as life slowly drains from them. As we talk about new strategies and systems of war, we must remember that each battle comes at the expense of the men who fought it. And their numbers would now increase. Once more we are looking mainly at Europe because that is where the greatest developments in weaponry and tactics were taking place. But Europeans had no monopoly on fighting: wars were being fought everywhere that human beings lived. We will eventually look at developments outside of Europe.

Europe in the seventeenth century was a continent in change. Remember that during medieval times a king was not exactly the head of a nation, as we think of it today. He was instead the holder of a piece of property called England, Bavaria, or Burgundy. Such a ruler might hold other pieces of property elsewhere, as the early English kings held towns and provinces in France.

But the idea of the nation—with the people who lived there not merely vassals and serfs, but citizens with common loyalties and certain rights—was growing. War was becoming not simply the business of kings and queens, but national affairs that concerned patriotic citizens.

Europe was marked by rivalries. These were partly the result of commercial competition: nations were growing rich from trade and wanted access to ports, raw materials, and new outlets for their products. A second important situation was the religious movement known as the Reformation. Since the fifteenth century and even earlier, some people had been objecting to certain practices of the powerful Roman Catholic Church, which held sway throughout Europe. Many believed that the church had become too concerned with power and wealth at the expense of its religious mission. They wanted to "purify" the church, or even set up competing Protestant religions. In other cases politics entered in; England banned the Roman Catholic Church in the sixteenth century because Henry VIII wanted to throw off the power of the pope. Rulers and whole nations began to take sides in the conflict between the Protestant and Roman Catholic faiths, and often there was war. And there were always the ambitions and envies of powerful men: everywhere princes, kings, or emperors were looking for opportunities for gain, to thwart a rival prince, or to defend themselves from attack. As a consequence during the seventeenth and eighteenth centuries war was almost continuous in Europe in one place or another. No victory was ever enough; no defeat was ever final. Periods of "peace" came only when national treasuries were empty.

It has been pointed out that there was a positive side to this endless warfare. The need for weaponry forced technological innovation, and the development of industries such as mining and metalworking in many ways improved the economies of the warring nations. But there was tremendous waste as well, not only in suffering and human life, but in material goods, as cities were bombarded and powder, metal, cloth, and much else were used up.

THIS SEVENTEENTH-CENTURY MUSKETEER IS EQUIPPED WITH TWELVE CARTRIDGES, A BULLET POUCH, A SWORD, AND A MATCHLOCK MUSKET. NOTE HOW HE HOLDS THE FLAMING END OF THE FUSE READY TO RELIGHT THE OTHER END IF NECESSARY. HE WEARS NO ARMOR, AS THE FORCE OF FIREARMS WAS TOO POWERFUL FOR ORDINARY ARMOR TO DEFLECT.

THIS EARLY BAYONET WAS FITTED OVER THE MUZZLE OF A GUN AFTER IT HAD BEEN FIRED, ATTACHED IN THE MOMENTS JUST PRECEDING A CHARGE.

As we have seen, throughout this period there was a steady improvement in weaponry. One new weapon of particular importance was the bayonet. The term had been used for daggers in the 1500s and may have been derived from the town of Bayonne, France, where such weapons first appeared. By about 1640 there existed an early form of bayonet, which had a tapering handle and plugged into the muzzle of a gun. The gun could not be fired with the bayonet in. To avoid this, a socket was eventually attached to the bayonet, which could be slid over the gun barrel. Bayonets were usually triangular in shape, intended for stabbing rather than cutting like a knife.

Warfare was now largely a matter of massive firepower, followed by a bayonet charge. Generally speaking, troops were formed in two or three rows; each fired in turn, reloaded, then fired again. As a rule the attacking army would come within reasonable firing range of the enemy, let loose one or more volleys, and then charge with fixed bayonets. The defenders would hold their fire until the attackers were within easy firing range, fire as often as they could until the attackers were upon them, and then fight with bayonets. By the eighteenth century troops were expected to be able to load and fire within fifteen seconds. This may seem fairly quick, but fifteen seconds can be a very long time when enemy troops are racing toward you with bayonets flashing.

Clearly in this kind of fighting it was important to have large numbers of troops in your army. Armies grew dramatically in size: in the sixteenth century a good-sized army might number in the tens of thousands; in the eighteenth century armies sometimes numbered in the hundreds of thousands. Discipline was also critically important: defenders had to stand fast in massive streams of bullets; attackers had to charge through the same.

Artillery, too, was important, for ranks of men standing shoulder to shoulder were easy pickings for cannoneers. Cavalry was stationed on the flanks, prepared to charge, swords waving, at a critical moment. But the heart of the new professional army was the foot soldier with his matchlock or flintlock, and his bayonet.

Given this arrangement, it was inevitable that most battles were fought on open plains and in fields. No longer was the primary object of war the taking of cities and towns, although that remained important; the key to victory was to destroy or at least cripple the enemy's fighting force.

This kind of fighting could not be done by farmers plucked from behind their plows, as had been the case in medieval times, when Edward III pulled together his army to fight in France. Soldiers needed long periods of training. They had to be disciplined so that they would stand firm in a rain of bullets, and they had to learn various types of marching movements so that on command they would race in formation from one part of a battlefield to the next as needed. Furthermore, nations needed to have men in military posts at their borders all year. As a result rulers created large "standing armies" made up of troops who were signed up for several years. Many of them were in fact forced into service by gangs of "press men" who picked up idlers and others off city streets.

Large standing armies could no longer depend on troops bringing their own swords, longbows, and pikes to camp. From then on each army would choose particular types of guns and swords. The government would see that the right equipment was manufactured in the necessary amounts and issue the items to the troops. The arms industry boomed and brought along with it related industries that produced textiles, shoes, and tents. Troops were issued standard uniforms, in part so soldiers could tell friend from enemy in battle, in part because handsome, colorful uniforms improved the spirits of soldiers.

These large standing armies could not be commanded by a single officer, as had been the case with Henry V at Agincourt. Armies were now broken down into successively smaller units, as they are today. Beginning with Gustavus Adolphus, about whom we will hear more shortly, permanent companies were made up of about a hundred men. Six to ten companies made up a battalion; two or three battalions composed a regiment; two to four regiments were in a brigade. Orders were passed down this chain of command from higher-ranking officers to lower ones. Soldiers were expected to instantly obey.

Not surprisingly, warfare became one of the principal preoccupations of European governments. Nations were frequently at war, and when they were not, they had to be prepared to fight, which meant feeding, clothing, and arming those large standing armies. One authority has said, "Just as the modern state was needed to create the standing army, so the army created the modern state, for the influence of the two causes was reciprocal." That is to say, standing armies could only be kept, and wars fought, by highly centralized governments that were able to control not only the armies and navies themselves, but the support industries, the national transportation and communications systems, and much else. War was now a state enterprise.

The man generally considered to be most responsible for creating the new European army of this period was Swedish king Gustavus Adolphus. He was born in 1594 and became King Gustavus II at the age of seventeen.

Gustavus had two primary interests to defend. For one, Sweden was mainly Protestant, so Gustavus felt he had a duty to support Protestant nations under attack by Catholic ones. For another, as an exporting nation, Sweden needed free use of the Baltic Sea and the ports around it. He was quite willing to send his army out to fight for these things.

Sweden was a relatively powerful nation at the time, but it was smaller than some others in Europe and had to make up in intelligence what it lacked in manpower. Part of Gustavus's genius lay in his attention to detail. He saw to it, for example, that his troops had warm uniforms, which not every leader bothered about. He worked out a careful system of supply, so that the soldiers would always have what they needed in order to fight. He worked out a simplified loading drill for muskets, something most commanders would have left to subordinates. Nothing escaped his eye, and his obvious concern for the well-being of his troops made them loyal to him and willing to fight.

In 1630 Gustavus decided to join in the Thirty Years' War, which had been going on since 1618. The causes of the war were complex, but the feuding between Protestants and Catholics was important. The armies supporting Catholicism had great initial successes and moved into northern Germany, which was basically Protestant. Gustavus brought his army across the Baltic and met the enemy forces at a place called Breitenfeld. With brilliant tactics, he maneuvered his infantry against the enemy, blunting their attack and then turning them back. Finally, at the critical moment, he led his own cavalry up a slope in a charge headed straight for the enemy's artillery. The horsemen broke through the line and captured the enemy cannon, which it now turned against them. Enemy resistance collapsed. In the Battle of Breitenfeld and others that followed, Gustavus kept northern Germany Protestant, which it remains today. This success and others persuaded kings and generals of other nations to study Gustavus's methods—not just his tactics in battle, but his attention to the details of supply and weaponry.

We are going to look at the effects of European weapon technology on the rest of the world in more detail in the next chapter. Here we need to look at a European rivalry that sloshed over into what would soon be the United States of America—and indeed played a major role in bringing that nation into being. The French and English had long been rivals, but by the eighteenth century the rivalry had become intense. Much of it had to do with competition for colonies overseas. In the New World, the French claimed what is now Canada, Louisiana, and especially Louisiana's capital, New Orleans. With both ends of the Mississippi River in its power, France wanted to gain control of the whole length of the river, which would give it a route for the shipment of trade goods, such as furs, out of huge areas of North America. We remember that at that time most transportation, especially in the North American wilderness, was by water.

The British, however, held the thirteen colonies ranged along the Atlantic coast from Georgia to what is now Maine. Neither the British overlords in London nor the colonists in America wanted the French to gain control of the lands across the Allegheny Mountains, especially the fertile Ohio Territory. Colonists were already pushing across the mountains to hunt for furs, claim land for speculation, and clear the forests for farms. The French were trying to keep them out, partly by encouraging the Indians to frighten off the colonists, and partly by building their own forts at key points, such as river junctions.

In 1756 a war known in Europe as the Seven Years' War broke out. It quickly spread to North America, where it is known as the French and Indian War. The British decided to make an effort to seize French lands in North America. They were supported by the Americans, who wanted to stop the French from encouraging the Indians to attack western settlements.

The British formulated a three-pronged plan. One force would push west from Virginia to take the French Fort Duquesne at the head of the Ohio River. Another prong would move north from Ticonderoga in upstate New York, over the Lake George–Lake Champlain waterway, aimed for the French colonial capital, Quebec. A third force, also aimed at Quebec, would sail up the Saint Lawrence River.

The first prong, after some tough fighting, took Fort Duquesne. It was renamed Fort Pitt, after the celebrated British prime minister William Pitt. The city that grew up there is now Pittsburgh. The second force, attempting to make its way north from Ticonderoga, got stalled.

The third expedition was commanded by a strange, often irascible, and sometimes sickly British officer named James Wolfe. It was now his task to take Quebec. The fate of North America would hang on the battle, for if the British could take Quebec, all of Canada and the head of the Mississippi would stand open to them.

But taking Quebec would be no easy job. The city was set atop a cliff 350 feet (107 m) above the Saint Lawrence River. The beach at the base of the cliff was narrow, leaving little room for attacking troops to land on. They would then have to scale the rock cliff to reach the city anyway.

In June 1759 Wolfe and his forces reached the Quebec area. Wolfe encamped his troops across the river from the city and bombarded it. Several times he attempted to land men somewhat to the east of the city, but the attempts always failed. The French were commanded by an excellent general, the Marquis de Montcalm. Each time Montcalm repelled the British advances.

Weeks passed. Finally some of Wolfe's junior officers convinced him that an attempt had to be made to attack Quebec from the west, up the steep rocky cliff. Wolfe began to study the cliff with his field glasses. One day he suddenly noticed a narrow path running up the cliff. If, somehow, he could take the French by surprise, he might be able to get enough troops up the path to the top of the cliff to fight a battle. It was, however, a desperate gamble: if the French discovered the British while they were still scrambling upward, they could be picked off with ease.

On September 13, at four in the morning, Wolfe's troops slipped into boats under the strictest orders of silence. With muffled oars the boats were rowed across the river. The soldiers silently disembarked, and some began making their way up the steep cliff, some along the path, and some scrambling from one handhold of rock or brush to the next. The French, assuming that the path was impassable, had left it lightly guarded. When day broke, the French discovered ranks of redcoats standing across a piece of flat ground by the city walls. This area was called the Plains of Abraham, and it would shortly be the site of one of the most significant battles ever fought in North America.

Wolfe and Montcalm each had about 4,500 troops, but Wolfe's men were well-trained British regulars, while many of Montcalm's men were local farmers hastily drawn into service. However, Montcalm felt he had no choice but to fight. His supplies were running low, and he had to drive the British army away.

At ten in the morning Montcalm, mounted on his horse, brought his troops out of the city, arranged them in ranks, and started them toward the British, bayonets fixed, in the classic manner of European warfare of the day. Wolfe commanded his troops to hold their fire. The British troops held steady under French fire, as their comrades beside them fell wounded or dead. Wolfe rushed among them encouraging them.

Finally, when the French were fifty yards (46 m) away, Wolfe gave the order to fire. The fusillade was devastating. The French line collapsed under the hail of fire, men screaming as they fell. The remainder of the French broke ranks and ran. The British then made a bayonet charge, and soon the demoralized French army was pinned against the city wall. Very quickly Montcalm called for a surrender. James Wolfe, however, had been shot in the chest, and within a few minutes he died. Montcalm, too, had been hit and died the next day.

It had been a classic eighteenth-century infantry battle. Cannons had

THIS ROMANTICIZED ILLUSTRATION SHOWS GEORGE WASHINGTON AT THE BATTLE OF MONONGAHELA DURING THE FRENCH AND INDIAN WAR. FOUR BULLETS PASSED THROUGH WASHINGTON'S COAT, AND TWO HORSES WERE SHOT FROM UNDER HIM. WASHINGTON'S BRAVERY WAS LEGENDARY.

been of minimal use, and there had been no cavalry action at all. It had lasted only for a morning, yet the consequences would be enormous. With Quebec in British hands, the French were finished in Canada. In the subsequent peace treaty, which settled both the American and European aspects of the war, the British got the vast territory of Canada. The Indians, without the French to encourage and supply them, became far less aggressive in their attacks on the western settlers. This in turn meant that Americans were less dependent on the mighty British army for protection. Soon many Americans, although hardly all, began to think that they no longer needed to stay within the shelter of the great and still growing British Empire, but could fend for themselves. Why pay taxes to the government in London? Why not govern themselves? In this way, the Battle on the Plains of Abraham led directly to the American Revolution and all that followed from it.

The American Revolution also began as an eighteenth-century war featuring massed infantry attacking each other in classic formations. George Washington, who had been given command of the American armies at the beginning of the Revolution, had been trained in this European system. But most Americans had had more experience fighting Indians than any other enemy, and Indian warfare was always a matter of surprise attack rather than of massed formations charging one another. At the Battle of Long Island, near the beginning of the war, the inexperienced Americans, unused to standing firm under pressure, broke and ran, and if the British had taken advantage of the victory, they might have ended the Revolution then and there. However, Washington had learned his lesson. He recognized that his poorly trained, poorly equipped troops could not stand up to the highly professional British armies. From then on he would avoid precisely planned battles, but depend on surprise. In the meanwhile he would duck and dodge until he had the advantage. As students of history know, one of his most celebrated victories came after the midnight crossing of the Delaware River, when his troops burst into Trenton, New Jersey, with fixed bayonets and swept the enemy before them.

In time the Americans learned the European system of warfare. The war was effectively ended by a standard attack. In 1780 the British major general Lord Cornwallis found himself bottled up at Yorktown, Virginia, a small

Practical Experience with Old Weapons

Readers of this book should not have to be told that experimenting at home with gunpowder is exceedingly dangerous, as many thousands of people missing a hand or blind in one eye have learned to their sorrow. Even today, specialist companies that make old-fashioned black gunpowder for firearms hobbyists sometimes have accidents. If professional manufacturers have problems with gunpowder, we can assume that amateurs experimenting at home are likely to have worse ones.

However, readers interested in getting hands-on experience with the original gunpowder and some of the older weapons described in this book will find several organizations to help them. For one, there are a number of groups around the country that stage regular re-enactments of historical battles, especially from the American Revolution and the Civil War. These groups wear historically accurate uniforms, carry flintlocks and percussion-cap guns, and retrace the course of major battles. A local historical society should have information on such groups.

There are also clubs that are primarily interested in competitive target shooting with black-powder weapons. In addition, many states have special hunting seasons for black-powder hunters. Any local hunting club will have information about black-powder hunting. The local police department or game warden can help, too.

Perhaps the best source of information on black-powder shooting is the National Muzzle Loading Rifle Association. This organization has programs specifically tailored for young people. It includes muzzle-loading clubs all over the United States, although there may not necessarily be one within easy driving range of every locality. These muzzle-loading clubs generally have instructional programs for students where they can work with old guns under supervision. Needless to say, students should discuss such activities with their parents first.

city that backed on the Potomac River. The French had come into the war on the side of the Americans, mostly in order to discomfort their old rivals, the British. For once, the French and American troops were considerably stronger than the British cornered in Yorktown. Cornwallis, a clever general, hoped to hold off the Americans and French until an expected British fleet arrived in the Potomac, which could take his men out of the trap they were in.

The Americans and French slowly ground forward, taking outposts and strongholds one at a time in hand-to-hand fighting. They kept up a heavy pounding of cannons into the city. Still Cornwallis held up; but when ships sailed into the Potomac River, they turned out to be French rather than English. There is a story told that when the serious-minded George Washington realized that it was the French fleet that was coming, not the British, he began leaping up and down on the dock, waving his large hat—a sight his fellow officers never forgot. Cornwallis surrendered, and the American Revolution was over, although it would be three years before the peace treaty was negotiated and signed.

THE BROWN BESS WAS A BRITISH FLINTLOCK WIDELY USED BY AMERICANS DURING THE REVOLUTIONARY WAR. THE ORIGIN OF THE NAME IS UNKNOWN, BUT IT WAS MUCH ADMIRED BY SOLDIERS.

This type of warfare, with masses of men alternately attacking each other, would, despite considerable changes, remain the model for combat into the twentieth century, when new rapid-fire weapons once again changed the face of combat.

A SECTION OF THE HULL OF THE H.M.S. *VICTORY*, ADMIRAL HORATIO NELSON'S FAMOUS FLAGSHIP, SHOWS IT BRISTLING WITH THREE ROWS OF CANNONS. THE CANNONS LINED BOTH SIDES OF THE SHIP AND COULD RELEASE A DEVASTATING BROADSIDE. ONLY THE EUROPEANS HAD VESSELS SUCH AS THESE, WHICH ALLOWED THEM NOT ONLY TO COMMAND THE SEAS, BUT TO EASILY DOMINATE PORTS IN CHINA, CENTRAL AMERICA, AND ELSEWHERE.

Europeans Export Their Weapons

Europeans had no monopoly on war. As we have seen, human beings have always fought everywhere they have existed. In the seventh century the Muslims under Muhammad and his successors conquered a huge swath of the world ranging from the edges of China, through the Middle East, across North Africa and into Spain. They held this vast empire for 700 years. For American Indian tribes, war was commonplace, a sort of deadly sport the men regularly engaged in. Tribal warfare in Africa was often waged for the purpose of taking prisoners, who were then often sold into slavery. The Chinese over their long history were again and again conquered or were conquering their neighbors. In some periods the Japanese had a strongly militaristic culture. No people have long spared themselves from war. The difference was that the Europeans had developed superior weapons.

Although some European travelers had visited other parts of the world earlier, the fifteenth century saw a sharp increase in European explorations of the world around them. They had ships that, however small they seem to us today, were at the time larger and more capable of enduring long journeys on the open sea than were the ships of other cultures. The

Portuguese were among the first to go regularly to distant places, first sailing their ships down the west coast of Africa, and then around the Cape of Good Hope into Asia. In 1492, as we know, Christopher Columbus, looking for "the Indies," ran into the Caribbean Islands instead.

These exploratory trips were partly made out of a spirit of adventure, but behind them was an ancient drive—wealth. Enterprising Europeans quickly understood that certain goods that were rare and expensive in Europe were plentiful and cheap elsewhere: silk and tea from China, spices from what is now Indonesia and nearby lands, lumber and furs from North America, gold and silver from Mexico and Peru, ebony and ivory from Africa, and much else.

Initially these seafarers went out mainly as traders, swapping manufactured goods such as clocks and guns—which most of the rest of the world lacked—for what the Europeans wanted. But it quickly became clear that with their advantage in weapons, the Europeans could simply take what they wanted. From there they went on to colonize great chunks of Asia, Africa, and the Americas.

The story of the European colonization of large portions of the world is huge and complex, and we can only touch on it briefly in a book of this size. The colonizing process followed several patterns. We will look at a few examples of several types as typical of the whole.

The beginning of European colonization is usually considered to be the taking of the port of Ceuta on the Strait of Gibraltar by the Portuguese in 1415. Over the next hundred years the Europeans established trading bases, and then colonies, in Africa, India, and various of the Pacific nations.

Best known to Americans, however, is the conquest of Mexico and Central, and much of South, America by Spain, in the process smashing the societies of the Aztecs, Incas, and Mayans. The most famous—or infamous—of the conquistadors was Hernán Cortés, a cruel, ambitious, but brave, even foolhardy fighter, who brought down the Aztec Empire and took over what is now roughly Mexico for Spain.

The Aztecs had a rich civilization with their own forms of art, a complex religion, and an even more complicated calendar system. They had built a

THIS CONTEMPORARY DRAWING SHOWS INDIANS DELIVERING GOLD AND JEWELRY TO THEIR SPANISH CONQUERORS. SPAIN AND, LATER, OTHER NATIONS DREW ENORMOUS WEALTH FROM THEIR COLONIES.

local empire by conquest and practiced human sacrifice to assuage the anger of their gods. However, they were not as technologically advanced as the Europeans. They did not use wheeled vehicles, but traveled most often by canoe on lakes and rivers. They had a form of picture writing, but no real alphabet. They had pottery and weaving, but by the time Cortés arrived had only rudimentary skill in working metal, used mainly in making thousands of gold ornaments, art objects, cups, and plates.

Their fighting technique was equally basic, consisting for the most part of the melee, in which masses of warriors charged one another to engage in hand-to-hand combat. Their failure to employ tactics in the European sense would cost them.

In the early 1500s the Aztecs began to hear rumors of strange light-skinned monsters who appeared to have four legs and the bodies of people rising from their backs. These were the Spanish soldiers of Cortés mounted on horses, animals the Aztecs had never seen. The Aztec leader, Montezuma, sent out ambassadors to meet the strangers and discovered that they were people much like themselves. Nonetheless, the Aztecs remained extremely worried: the newcomers appeared to have godlike attributes and clearly were going to be hard to appease. Making matters worse, in the year prior to the arrival of Cortés and his soldiers, a number of ominous signs and portents had appeared—strange fires, inexplicable bolts of lightning without thunder, a woman's voice crying out, "My children, we are lost." The Aztecs, especially Montezuma, were unnerved.

Montezuma had less fantastic problems as well. His empire was not unified, as the Roman Empire had been, with one strong leader at its head. It consisted of a very loose confederation of city-states, in which the chiefs of the member states coveted their own power, and had to be constantly wooed by Montezuma. Many of them would be happy to escape from Montezuma's dominance. As Cortés marched through these little princedoms toward the great Aztec capital, Tenochtitlán, he played upon these rivalries. He sometimes persuaded some of the princes—at least for a short period of time—to ally themselves with him against Montezuma. By the time Cortés reached the Aztec capital, Montezuma was so uncertain of what to do that the Spanish walked in unmolested and took Montezuma hostage.

HERE, INDIANS BATTLE WITH BOWS AND CLUBS AGAINST EUROPEANS EQUIPPED WITH GUNS, SWORDS, AND SHIELDS. EUROPEAN DISEASES WERE ONE OF THE MAJOR REASONS THE CONQUEST OF THE NEW WORLD WAS SO SWIFT AND SUCCESSFUL, BUT THE USE OF WEAPONS WAS ANOTHER CRITICAL ADVANTAGE.

The Aztecs had difficulties in organizing a response, but eventually they managed to drive the Spanish out of Tenochtitlán, in the process killing three-quarters of the invaders.

Yet despite these devastating losses, wounds, and fatigue, the Spanish made a stand at a place called Otumba. Here they maintained their discipline and fought off a much larger force of Indians who resided in the area and were under the control of the Aztec Empire. At a crucial moment the remains of the Spanish cavalry, in European fashion, charged the enemy, reached their chiefs, and killed them all. Resistance collapsed, and the Indians fled.

Cortés then rested his troops and awaited reinforcements. When they had arrived he began to move systematically through various areas of Mexico, sometimes with the help of Indian allies, taking town after town. The Indians found it difficult to stand up to Spanish weapons and tactics, and resistance never lasted very long.

Then, with a solid base and many Indian allies, Cortés set out to attack Tenochtitlán. The city was built on an island in a large lake. Cortés arranged to have a fleet of small boats built and carried in. Soldiers in this little fleet, with their guns, quickly cleared the lake of Aztec canoes. Other Indian groups, smelling victory and spoils, joined the Spanish. The Spanish were still outnumbered, but their cannons, armor, swords, and muskets eventually overpowered the Aztecs, and in time Tenochtitlán fell.

For the next 300 years, Mexico would be a province of Spain, ruled by Spanish officials sent from Madrid, whose main job was to exploit Mexico and its people for the good of Spain. Over time the Mexican Indians interbred with the Spanish, and sometimes blacks, to the point where pure-blooded Indians in Mexico are today a minority. The Spanish imposed on the Aztecs and other Mexicans a European culture—the Spanish language; the Roman Catholic religion; European weapons and fighting methods, art, and literature. And yet, says one scholar, "Though their outward aspect and their material and social culture are European, the stamp of the Aztec character is on their minds, just as the masonry of broken Aztec temples is built into the walls of their churches."

The colonization of Mexico and other Spanish domains was a complete takeover, with the conquerors at the top and the native population largely reduced to serfdom, or in some cases outright slavery. The colonization of North America followed a different pattern.

In the late 1500s the English, under their revered Queen Elizabeth I, were increasingly troubled by the rapidly growing wealth of the Spanish, much of it coming from their colonies. At the time, Spain was a great rival of the English. Among other things, the Spanish were Roman Catholics. The English had recently left the Catholic Church, and Spanish rulers believed they had a duty to bring the English back to Rome. Furthermore, the Spanish wished to put an upstart rival in its place.

The English believed that they had to protect themselves against the Spanish, in part by obtaining colonies of their own, but Elizabeth was by nature cautious and slow to get her nation moving. When she did send out explorers, they did not succeed in establishing settlements.

In 1603 a new ruler, James I, made another effort. By this time the English were seriously concerned that they were being left out of the scramble for riches in the Americas. Moreover, they were suffering from what appeared to be overpopulation: for reasons too complex to get into here, a great many English people, including many children, had been driven out of farms and villages and found themselves in cities, especially London, without work. They begged, stole, drank, and otherwise caused trouble. The best solution, according to the English rulers, would be to ship the unemployed out to colonize the New World.

In early 1607 three ships set out for what had been called Virginia, after Elizabeth, the Virgin Queen. On board were some gentlemen who did not really expect to work in Virginia; some adventurers looking for profits; and a good many indentured servants, who were little more than slaves, although the term of their service was limited, usually to seven years.

The English—indeed Europeans in general—were woefully ignorant of the Indian society they were about to confront. The Indian cultures of North America were exceedingly diverse: the tribes of the Southwest with their pueblos and corn-based economy lived quite differently from the Northwest Indians who hunted whales from great wooden dugout canoes. The Indians of the Virginia area were a rich and prosperous people who grew corn, beans, squash, and other crops, but also hunted deer and gathered shellfish in the coastal waters. Like many Indian groups, they were always forming and re-forming alliances of various kinds, and getting into and out of wars, usually brief.

At the time the English arrived in 1607, much of the area around Virginia was under the loose control of a strong leader named Powhatan, who had put together a federation of tribes that regularly paid him tribute. The Indians in many places in the Americas had, over the previous hundred years, suffered heavy losses of population from diseases brought by Europeans, such as measles and smallpox, to which the Europeans were at least partially immune. Nonetheless, the Powhatan group amounted to perhaps 12,000 people, more than enough to drive out a few hundred English. When the English first arrived in April 1607, the Indians attacked. They were driven off by cannon fire from the ships.

The English then set about building a palisaded fort at a place they called Jamestown, after the English king. A group went off to find the Indians and explain that they had come in peace. While the scouting party was gone, the Indians attacked again, and once again were driven off from the ships by cannon fire. Then, however, the ships sailed back to England.

But the disease problem worked both ways. Quickly the English began to fall ill from diseases and a climate they were unused to, and when food began to run out, from starvation as well. Within weeks the colony was down to thirty-eight people. At this point Powhatan could easily have wiped out the colony. But he was not sure he wanted to: among other things, he thought that he might be able to bring English guns in on his side against local enemies. In part, too, the Indians remained somewhat fearful of gunpowder weapons, mostly because of the noise and smoke they made, which seemed somehow miraculous. Whatever his reasons, for the moment Powhatan stayed his hand and gave the colonists fish, meat, and corn, which enabled them to struggle on. Eventually ships with supplies and additional colonists arrived, and the colony staggered on through 1608 and 1609.

But relations with the Indians were going downhill. It is hard to pin down precisely who was to blame. The settlers were now occasionally raiding Indian villages for corn, but it is also true that Indians were inclined to pick off stray colonists who wandered too far from home. Powhatan decided to besiege the little colony. Soon the starving English were eating dogs, rats, mice, and eventually the corpses of their dead fellows. When a ship arrived from the West Indies in May 1610, the man in charge was so shocked by the condition of the colonists that he ordered Jamestown abandoned. He was actually loading them aboard his ship when a new ship sailed up the James River bearing food, supplies, 150 new colonists, and 100 soldiers.

Over the next few years, an uneasy peace was maintained, with occasional raids and killings on both sides. It was discovered that there were riches to be made in growing tobacco. Tobacco farms spread up and down the James River. Little villages grew. Slowly the English colony grew stronger.

Finally Powhatan died in an epidemic. The new chief was more aggressive than Powhatan had been and decided to wipe out the colony once and for all. In 1622 he struck hard, sending warriors into tobacco farms and villages, killing 347 men, women and children—about a third of the colony.

If the Indians had followed with an attack on Jamestown itself, they might have driven the English into the sea. They did not. They were used to Indian warfare, in which a badly beaten enemy usually became discouraged and gave up. The English, however, decided to drive the Indians away. Sixty armed men dressed in breastplates marched into Indian territory, where they were met by 800 Indians in an open field. For two days the Indians fought with valor, but their bows had not been designed to penetrate armor, but for use in wooded areas against deer and unarmored humans. Their arrows bounced off English helmets and breastplates. A great many Indians were killed by English guns; only sixteen colonists were wounded and none died.

The battle broke the Powhatan confederation. Indians from other tribes who had witnessed the fight took home the lesson that the English could not be beaten, no matter how badly outnumbered. Thereafter the Virginia colony—based on tobacco and eventually slave labor—bloomed, and step by step the Indians were pushed back.

Here then, was a second colonial pattern: whereas the Spanish in Mexico and elsewhere tended to turn the native populations into serfs, the English in North America generally drove them out. When Massachusetts was settled beginning in 1620, after a few at-

THIS RE-ENACTMENT OF LIFE IN THE JAMESTOWN SETTLEMENT SHOWS AN ARMED MAN STANDING GUARD AGAINST POSSIBLE INDIAN ATTACK, WHILE OTHERS WORK THE FIELDS. THE HOSTILITY BETWEEN INDIANS AND THE ENGLISH SETTLERS ONLY ENDED WHEN THE INDIANS WERE FINALLY DRIVEN FROM THEIR LANDS.

tempts to live peaceably together, the English settlers concluded that they had to drive the Indians away. And so it went for 250 years, until the Indians were finally confined to reservations and their land belonged to the newcomers. It is true, of course, that a considerable part of the problem was the diseases the Europeans brought with them, which killed far more Indians than bullets ever did, but the policy of the North American colonists was nonetheless to claim the land for themselves, mainly for farming.

The way that China was dominated by the West followed a third pattern. China is an old society. People identifiable as Chinese were living in North China by Neolithic times, and by about 1500 B.C. were working with bronze. By 500 B.C. and perhaps earlier, China had walled cities, a feudal society, and inevitably, warfare. At times strong rulers were able to unify parts or all of the country and hold it together through a large and often unwieldy bureaucracy; at other times the country splintered into competing tribal domains.

By the thirteenth century, when European technology was beginning to move forward, the Chinese had built the first clock, although they had not gone on to build another one, and they had also invented gunpowder. In that century Marco Polo, a Venetian, spent time in China and wrote about it, whetting European appetites for more information. For a period thereafter, the Chinese welcomed European visitors, but eventually a strong desire to avoid foreign influence took over, and rules were set up to keep Westerners out. The Chinese believed that they had the world's most superior culture and that they had nothing to learn from the blue-eyed barbarians from the West.

Nonetheless, they were fascinated by Western technology, such as clocks and gunpowder weapons, which they saw the value of. Europeans were increasingly interested in opening up China for trade, because products such as silk, tea, and porcelain could be sold in Europe for great sums of money. (We still use the word *china* for plates and dishes.) Chinese rulers were torn, and gradually they let European traders gain small footholds. In 1557 Portugal established the trading city of Macao on a peninsula jutting out into the South China Sea. (Macao remained a Portuguese possession until very recently, when it was returned to China.) Portugal quickly gained a monopoly of the Chinese trade. Roman Catholic priests followed the Portuguese, and soon Catholic missionaries were trying to establish themselves in China. On a few occasions the Chinese also let in Western scholars and craftsmen who could be useful to the Chinese, such as the German Schall von Bell, who revised the Chinese calendar and cast cannons for the government.

Inevitably other envious European governments tried to break the Portuguese monopoly of China's trade. By the eighteenth century many European nations, and eventually the United States, were beginning to trade with China. However, the Chinese still refused to let the foreigners travel freely about the country. Traders were confined to the port city of Canton (now called Guangzhou), where they built their warehouses, offices, and dwellings along a narrow stretch of waterfront, which they were not supposed to leave. Chinese officials consistently treated European traders as their inferiors, a low class of sordid merchants. Nonetheless, there were profits to be made all around, and the trade was tolerated by the Chinese.

The European traders wanted to be able to move freely around China to do business with merchants and manufacturers directly, instead of being confined to Canton. Friction was particularly intense between the Chinese and the British. Drinking tea had become a great fad in England, and the British were importing a tremendous amount of tea. They had been paying for it by selling opium to the Chinese, which they brought in from India. The Chinese were worried that the drug was demoralizing the Chinese people and tried to stop the opium trade. The English considered this an unreasonable restraint on their rights, and protested. Soon thereafter the Opium War broke out in 1839. The English, with their vastly superior gunboats, had no trouble winning a string of victories, and in 1842 the Chinese gave up and signed a treaty that gave the British Hong Kong, opened other ports to British trade, and legalized the opium trade. A second war beginning in 1856 forced the Chinese to live up to the earlier agreement.

The Chinese now saw the way events were heading. In the 1860s and 1870s a new group of leaders outlined a new policy: China would keep its old Confucian ideals of social harmony, but would import Western technology. However, anti-Western feeling remained strong, and in 1900 a "disorganized mass" of peasants known as the Boxers besieged the foreign quarter of the capital, Peking (now called Beijing). In response European and American troops marched in and quickly suppressed the Boxers.

Western leaders were now determined that China would be open to trade with everybody, no matter what the Chinese thought about it. The

West had the guns, the cannons, the ever-larger battleships, and there was really nothing the Chinese could do to prevent it. The failure of the Chinese to develop their technology had proven costly indeed.

The Chinese people were not forced into serfdom as the Mexicans had been or driven off the land like the North American Indians. China was too big and too populous to make a complete takeover attempt worthwhile or possible. Nonetheless, as far as trade went, China would be economically dominated by Westerners until 1949, when the Communists took over and threw up a wall around China that only today is being breached.

There were other colonial systems besides these three. Each new colony had to have a governing system customized by the European colonists to suit local conditions. But these three patterns were important ones.

It should be remembered, of course, that Europeans were not the first to colonize other peoples, or the last. The Mongols, under Genghis Khan and his successors, built an empire that stretched for a thousand miles across central Asia, at a time when Europeans were still squabbling over small

EUROPEAN TROOPS ARE SHOWN APPROACHING THE FORBIDDEN CITY, THE CENTRAL PALACE IN BEIJING, CHINA'S CAPITAL, WHICH WAS THEN KNOWN AS PEKING. THE ANTI-EUROPEAN BOXER REBELLION WAS QUICKLY SNUFFED OUT, AND FOREIGN POWER IN CHINA INCREASED.

principalities. As we have seen, even earlier the Muslims built an even larger empire that stretched into Europe. And as late as the 1940s, the Japanese colonized huge chunks of the lands around the Pacific Ocean.

But the colonization of a good deal of the world by the West in the years 1500 to 1900 has had lasting effects. During the twentieth century, especially as a consequence of the world wars of 1914–1918 and 1939–1945, most of the colonies threw off their European rulers. By the 1960s, if not earlier, the great colonies of Germany, France, Italy, England, and Spain were mostly independent.

Yet Western ideas, art, popular culture (much of it stemming from the United States), and especially technology have been absorbed by nations around the world. Some of the best performers of European symphonic music, especially violin players, are Chinese and Japanese. Jazz can be heard in Indonesia and Malaysia. European sports such as soccer, tennis, and golf are played all around the world. Western-style dress, ranging from suits and ties to blue jeans and sneakers, has been adopted in Pakistan, Somalia, and Uzbekistan. Perhaps most importantly, parliamentary democracy, which was mainly created in Europe, is today being tried, however cautiously, in dozens of nations that only a half century ago were ruled by despots. But even more popular than Western clothes and music in the rest of the world is Western hardware—missiles, jet fighters, and tanks.

To be sure, there is resistance to Western ideas and culture. Some groups of Muslims wish to fight off Western influence, banning television and Western dress in their countries, as the Taliban did in Afghanistan. Small pockets of American Indians have kept alive their ancient religions and at least some of their folkways. Despite the popularity of European suits in business circles, East Indians continue to wear traditional saris.

But at this point, resistance appears to be a losing battle, although it is difficult to make guesses about the future. The culture developed in Europe and its descendants, such as the United States, Brazil, and Australia, is having a powerful influence worldwide. Without European superiority in weapons—the cannon, hard steel armor, the flintlock—it would not have happened.

Guerrier Iroquois.

An Iroquois Indian is about to scalp an enemy. Despite their adherence to their well-established warrior traditions, Indians generally adapted easily to the flintlocks they acquired from European settlers. This illustration was made by a Frenchman traveling in the United States in 1787.

The Beginnings of the Modern Army

Throughout the eighteenth century the faithful flintlock remained the standard weapon for both warfare and hunting. Not only was it used in European warfare, but it was adopted by the colonial people the Europeans were trying to subjugate. West African chieftains traded ebony, ivory, and—regrettably—slaves, for flintlocks. The American Indians were so pleased with the flintlock that a special version was manufactured for them, a simple, cheap weapon with a short barrel for ease of shooting on horseback or in the eastern woodlands. The Indians liked this weapon so much that they continued to use it until the end of the Indian wars even when newer types of guns became available.

But inevitably people were looking for ways to make the flintlock more accurate and faster to load. One particular problem was the slight delay that occurred between the moment the powder in the pan ignited and the powder in the barrel was fired. The delay was only a fraction of a second, but it meant that the shooter had to hold his aim just that much longer after he had pulled the trigger. For the bird hunter the delay meant that he had to lead, that is, shoot ahead of, his darting fowl a little more than he would have had to with a faster firing system. One hunter, a Scotsman named Alexander John Forsyth, noticed that fowl would instantly dive on seeing the flash in the pan. The firing delay was just enough to allow the bird to escape.

Forsyth was an avid sportsman who hunted waterfowl along the Scottish coast not far from his home near Aberdeen. He began hearing about a new explosive substance called fulminate. Fulminates were made by dissolving metals in acid. They had been made of gold, silver, and mercury, but not primarily for use as explosives. Forsyth set about seeing what he could do with fulminates to improve the firing speed of flintlocks. His key discovery was that fulminate would explode not only when it was lit like gunpowder, but when it was struck. This very simple idea would lead directly to modern guns of all kinds.

Eventually Forsyth worked out a system for firing the flintlock built around a hammer that struck a little fulminate. Forsyth's system was clearly faster than the old sparks-and-pan method, but it was expensive to make and not entirely reliable. Armies did not take it up, but continued to use the old flintlock.

However, Forsyth's fulminate system proved useful for sporting weapons. Many bird hunters were, like Forsyth, gentlemen who hunted as much for sport as for food, and could afford a more expensive gun. Furthermore they were willing to sacrifice a measure of reliability in exchange for firing speed, which was something a soldier faced with charging bayonets was unwilling to do. Others began trying to improve on Forsyth's idea. These efforts mainly involved mixing fulminate with a glue or binder and shaping it into pellets that could be inserted into a special nipple over the gun's chamber. When the trigger was pulled, a spring would drive a small hammer down onto the pellet, which would then explode and instantly fire the weapon.

Out of these experiments came the percussion cap, essentially a small container holding a small amount of fulminate covered with a disk of tinfoil and waterproofed with shellac. The cap was fitted over the nipple and was struck by a hammer to explode it. One great advantage of the percussion cap was that it could be fired in wet weather.

Once again, although the percussion cap was seized upon by sportsmen, armies were hesitant to take it up. For one thing, the time required to carefully fit the small cap onto the nipple actually made it slower to load

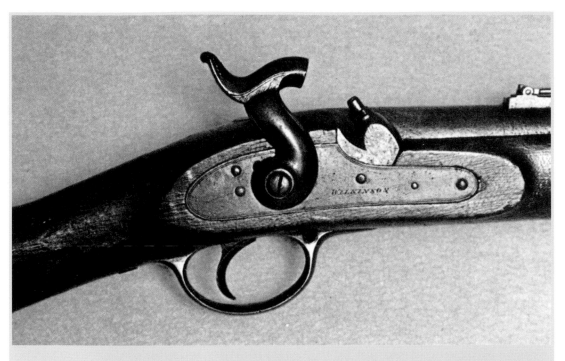

A PERCUSSION LOCK. THE PERCUSSION CAP FIT OVER THE NIPPLE AND FIRED WHEN IT WAS STRUCK BY THE HAMMER. THE EXPLODING CAP IN TURN IGNITED THE POWDER IN THE BARREL.

than the old flintlock. For another, frightened soldiers might find it difficult to put on the cap with bullets raining around them. Nonetheless, despite the disadvantages, the value of the percussion cap was clear, and by about 1830 the percussion-cap system was starting to be used by armies. The long day of the fabled flintlock, which had seen action in battles from the English Civil War in the 1600s to the American Indian wars of the 1800s, was finally over.

There was more innovation to come. It had long been known that a spinning projectile travels with less wobble or drift than one that does not spin. For this reason footballs are usually kicked and thrown so that they spin, or "spiral." A child's toy gyroscope works on the same principle: as long as it is spinning it will stand up. As far back as 1500 and perhaps earlier, feathers were attached to arrows at an angle to make them spin for greater stability in flight. The reason for this effect was not known: many people believed it to be the work of the devil, although the effect is of course due to a law of physics.

Inevitably people began to wonder if a bullet could be spun to make it travel straighter. By around 1500 it was discovered that the trick was to run spiral grooves along the inside of the barrel. If the ball was slightly larger than the diameter of the barrel, some of the lead would be squeezed into the grooves when the ball was forced home in loading. When the gun was fired, the ball would necessarily spin as it traveled down the barrel, and go on spinning on the way to the target. Gun makers thus began rifling barrels with perhaps six to twelve parallel spiral grooves.

But rifling had some serious drawbacks. For one, it took a good deal of pressure to force the ball down the bore, which took time, something armies could ill afford. For another, the groove quickly grew dirty, which meant that the barrel had to be swabbed clean after two or three shots so a new ball could be driven home.

But if the rifle could not be used as a military weapon except in special circumstances, it was eminently useful for hunting, where accuracy was the primary concern. Through the sixteenth and seventeenth centuries the rifle was increasingly used in Europe for hunting and for target-shooting contests, which were widely popular, sometimes drawing contestants from several countries.

Eventually—where, when, and by whom yet again we do not know—it was discovered that if a ball that fitted easily into the gun bore was wrapped in a small patch of cloth, the cloth could be squeezed into the grooves and would impart a spin to the ball as it traveled down the barrel. Patches were in use for rifles by 1600 and perhaps before. Patch-loading was much faster than the old system, and the patch itself helped to keep the bore clean. Nonetheless, the cheaper smoothbore remained the preferred weapon for armies: by 1700, if not before, armies were usually firing at close range where accuracy was not critical.

It was the Americans, more than any other group, who helped develop the rifle into a major weapon. In Europe, hunting was a sport largely practiced by the aristocracy and the wealthy, people who could afford expensive weapons and the hunting preserves many maintained for their private use. In America it was a different story: the gun was an essential piece of equipment for many families, especially those living on the frontier. Even well into the 1800s, game—especially deer and wild birds— was an important source of food for many farm families. In some places marauding wolves, foxes, cougars, and other animals were a constant threat to a farmer's livestock. And at times there was the fear of Indian raids. The need for a fast, accurate weapon was acute.

For a considerable period, the old smoothbore musket remained the primary weapon on the frontier and with farmers generally. Then in the seventeenth and eighteenth centuries, a substantial number of Swiss and Germans immigrated to the colony of Pennsylvania—the famous "Pennsylvania Dutch." (Dutch is a corruption of the word for German, *deutsche*). Germany had been an important center for the making of rifles. Many of the German immigrants were gunsmiths, and over time Pennsylvania Germans, among others, developed a rifle tailored to American needs. It had a long barrel for accuracy, a stock of durable curly maple, and a box in the stock to hold patches. Gradually this rifle replaced the old musket.

This famous rifle had been given many names: the American rifle, the long rifle, the Kentucky rifle, the Pennsylvania rifle. Americans grew extremely adept at using it. Boys and often girls learned to shoot as soon as they were old enough to hold a gun. The accuracy of this weapon became legendary. In some shooting contests participants were required to hit the head of a turkey at 250 feet (76 m), nearly the length of a football field.

During the American Revolution, when many troops brought their own arms, the rifle appeared on the battlefield.

THE FAMOUS KENTUCKY, OR LONG, RIFLE. THE LONGER BARREL ALLOWED FOR GREATER ACCURACY, BUT THE RIFLING, WHICH IMPARTED A SPIN TO THE BULLET, WAS KEY TO THE DEADLY PROWESS AMERICANS ACHIEVED WITH THIS WEAPON.

Tacticians discovered that it was useful to station a few expert riflemen among the regular infantry in order to shoot artillerymen and to pick off enemy officers who thought they were at a safe distance. In the end the artillery was forced to move back some distance behind their own troops to avoid the bullets of enemy riflemen.

But rifles were still too slow to load for ordinary military use. Furthermore they were not yet fitted with bayonets—although they could have been—which meant that when faced with an enemy charge, riflemen would have to flee once they had discharged one or two balls, as the bayonets of the enemy bore down on them.

The situation was improved in 1828 when a French officer, Captain Gustave Delvigne, designed a gun in which a loose-fitting ball was dropped down the barrel and then tamped with a ramrod enough to make it expand, thus pressing into the grooves. A second breakthrough came when various experimenters devised a cylindrical bullet with a cone-shaped head, which looked a good deal like a modern bullet. This bullet had a slightly hollow base. When the powder exploded into this hollow, it forced the base of the bullet to expand, jamming it tightly against the bore walls (the inside of the barrel) and into the spiral rifling.

With these innovations, more than 300 years after the advent of the rifle, there was a gun that could be loaded as fast as a smoothbore. The smoothbore faded quickly, and by the 1850s the new rifle was being adopted by armies everywhere. One of the most famous of these early army rifles was the Enfield, manufactured in Enfield, England. Many Enfield rifles were used by both sides in the American Civil War.

Some of these new bullets with hollow bases made a whistling sound as they raced through the air. They acquired the name Minié balls, from the name of one of the originators. Civil War soldiers found these "minny balls," as they termed them, fearful, and they grew to hate the whistling sound.

The percussion-cap rifle, especially in the hands of Americans who had been trained from youth to use it, was a considerably more deadly weapon than the old smoothbore flintlock, which was really effective only at close range. In fact, under the old system, infantrymen were not expected to aim carefully, which took too much time, but to fire as rapidly as possible to create a wall of flying lead through which attackers must attempt to charge. The accurate new rifle allowed defenders to begin slaughtering opponents while they were still a good distance away, indeed almost as soon as they came into sight. This meant that they might be under fire the entire time it took them to slog forward over a rough battlefield or the length of two or three football fields. The advantage was now passing back to the defense; but unfortunately it was a long time before the generals learned the lesson. During the American Civil War, while the generals were learning, 600,000 men were killed, more than those who died in any other war fought by Americans.

The Civil War is one of the most chronicled events in human history. The books on it number in the hundreds of thousands. Not only is it studied intensely in the United States, but students of military history everywhere analyze it for the lessons it contains. Even today cadets at military schools in China, France, and Russia study the battles of the American Civil War. It has been called "the first modern war," and while that may be an exaggeration, there is a good deal of truth in it.

The American Civil War was complex, fought over a much larger area than most wars of the time, by several armies that often were out of touch with each other. We can hardly give even a brief history of the war in a book of this size; we will try to touch on two or three key battles.

The aim of the Northern command was not so much to gain territory, but to destroy the Southern armies and force the Southern states back into the Union. The goals of the South were simply to keep the Northern armies out of its territory and inflict enough serious losses on them so that the people of the North would become discouraged, give up the fight, and allow the Southern Confederacy to become a nation of its own.

At first the South had the best of it: at set-piece battles (precisely planned and carried out) such as First Bull Run, Northern troops turned and ran. The Southern general, Robert E. Lee, concluded that any number of Southern troops could beat any number of Northern ones. It was a mistake.

CIVIL WAR SHARPSHOOTERS USING THE HIGHLY ACCURATE NEW RIFLES COULD KILL ENEMY SOLDIERS AT GREAT DISTANCES WHILE KEEPING THEMSELVES UNDER COVER. ALTHOUGH IT TOOK GENERALS A LONG TIME TO REALIZE IT, THE BALANCE HAD SHIFTED TO THE DEFENSE.

At Shiloh, at the western end of Tennessee, the North won a victory and used it to effectively gain control of the rest of the state.

One small fight at the time of Shiloh was a sign of things to come. At one point a surprise attack by the Confederate troops drove the Northern troops back. To hold them off temporarily, the Northern commander, General William Tecumseh Sherman, later famous for his devastating march through Georgia, ordered General Benjamin Prentiss to put together a defense in a patch of brush and trees, which the Confederates soon began to call the Hornet's Nest. Prentiss had only 4,500 men; the attacking Confederates were 18,000 strong. Fighting from under cover with only a few cannons, the Union soldiers held off charge after charge of Southern "maddened demons" and were forced to surrender only when they ran out of ammunition.

The fight at the Hornet's Nest should have made it clear that troops in fortified positions, equipped with the new rifles, could not be easily routed. One solder hidden in a ditch or behind a stone wall, firing two or more rounds a minute with an accurate weapon, could kill or disable a substantial number of attackers in the time it took them to race up a hill or across a field to get within bayonet range. But old ideas were deeply ingrained, and the lesson was not yet learned.

One man who in time learned the lesson was General Ulysses S. Grant, ultimately chief of the Union forces. After Shiloh, Grant went on to attack the city of Vicksburg on the Mississippi River. It was a key point, for it controlled traffic up and down the river, important to the Confederates for transporting supplies. If Grant and his Union forces could take Vicksburg, they could cut this supply line, gain control of the river, and thus sever the Confederacy from its western states. In the winter of 1862–1863, Grant isolated and surrounded Vicksburg. Again and again he sent his troops charging at the outnumbered Confederate soldiers in the city. But the defense could not be cracked. In the end Grant accepted this fact and settled down to besiege the city, which surrendered only when the Confederate defenders were starving and too sick and weak to fight.

But most generals took longer to learn, among them the Southern star, General Robert E. Lee. Not long before Vicksburg finally surrendered in the summer of 1863, Lee decided to carry the fight into the North. The Confederacy, which had never had a great industrial base, was always short of supplies. Lee knew that in prosperous Pennsylvania he might find barns full of livestock and warehouses full of shoes, rifles, or clothing. A solid victory might also help to shake Northern confidence. In addition, the British, who wanted Southern cotton for their textile mills, were thinking about supporting the South; a victory would convince them that the Confederacy was certain to win. The South hoped that the British would

THE CAPTION ON THIS DRAWING, MADE ON THE SCENE, READS, "THE BATTLE OF GETTYSBURG: VIEW FROM THE SUMMIT OF LITTLE ROUND TOP ON THE EVENING OF THURSDAY, JULY 2, 1863. REPULSE OF THE ATTACK OF LONGSTREET'S CORPS BY THE 5TH CORPS. SKETCHED ON THE SPOT. SUNDOWN. E. FORBES." EDWIN FORBES WAS PERHAPS THE GREATEST OF THE CIVIL WAR ARTISTS AND WAS FAMOUS IN HIS TIME.

then enter the war on its side. Lee remained convinced that his own men were vastly superior fighters to the Yankees.

Lee gathered his forces and began to move into Pennsylvania. Opposed to him was the Union general George Gordon Meade, who was determined to stop Lee. As the two armies maneuvered, looking for each other and an advantageous place to fight, a small force from each side bumped into one another near the little town of Gettysburg, where a number of roads came together.

The battle began immediately. Hastily Meade and Lee called in their forces. Even before all his troops had gathered, Lee, always eager to fight, called for an attack. The Confederates charged, shouting the fearsome rebel yell. The Union troops fell back onto high ground called Cemetery Ridge and dug in. It was a strong defensive position with a stone wall running along portions of it, and fields and orchards below it, offering a clear field of fire. As more troops on both sides arrived, Lee once again decided to launch an attack. One of the generals, James Longstreet, argued that the ridge could not be taken by a frontal attack. But Lee was adamant, and on the next day, July 2, 1863, Longstreet attacked. For hours the Confederate troops charged the Union position. Many times they drew close enough to the Union lines for bayonet fighting. Two or three times they pierced Union defenses only to be thrown back. By nightfall Cemetery Ridge was still in Union hands.

But Lee believed that he had almost broken through and that one last push would do it. He ordered Longstreet to prepare another charge for the next morning with three divisions totaling 15,000 men. Again Longstreet protested. "General," he is reported to have said, "there never was a body of fifteen thousand men who could make that attack successfully." But Lee insisted, and the next morning Longstreet ordered an artillery bombardment of the Northern position. Soon the Union guns fell silent, put out of action, so it seemed, by Confederate shells. Longstreet then sent his troops forward on a mile-long (1.6 km-long) front. Among them were fresh troops led by General George Pickett. The rebels started forward, and then the Union cannons began to sound; they had not been put out of action at all, and they mowed down the advancing Confederates like wheat.

Pickett's men came under especially heavy fire, but some of them actually managed to climb over a stone wall at a place on the ridge called the Angle. Desperate Union reinforcements drove them off. Soon the rebels were running back down the hill, where their comrades lay dying, heading for the cover of trees behind the field they had just crossed. In thirty minutes half of the brave 15,000 men had been killed or wounded. Lee went among the survivors, telling them that it had been his fault, as indeed it had been. In those three days at Gettysburg, the Union lost a quarter of the men it had there, the Confederates a third—53,000 men. Some historians have said that when Pickett's men climbed the wall at the Angle, the Confederacy had reached its high tide.

If Lee had not learned the lesson, Grant had. By the winter of 1864–1865, Grant had Lee bottled up at Petersburg, a town not far from the Confederate capital of Richmond. Petersburg was a key railroad junction; if the Union could take it, Richmond was sure to fall. Once again Grant tried a frontal assault, and when that failed, he settled into a siege to starve the Southerners out. Step by step he tightened the noose around the city, blocking roads and railroad lines to prevent the defenders from being supplied. In the end the desperate Lee broke loose and headed west, hoping to be able to turn south where he could join Confederate forces and regroup. But Grant kept moving with Lee, preventing him from turning. At the little town of Appomattox Courthouse, Lee gave up. The Civil War was over.

When the Civil War ended, the day of massed armies charging one another was over. New weapons had made a frontal attack a very deadly proposition. As one military historian puts it, "The solid infantry formations of earlier years disappeared; the old type of cavalry warfare, shock action against infantry, went out of business; the spade and the axe became necessary articles in battle; breastworks and rifle pits were used to give cover and protection."

And yet, as we will see in a later chapter, some generals still had not learned the lesson.

developments in arms would not have been possible. Hand operations could never have produced brass cartridges exact enough for machine guns running at high speed, nor could a factory have made by hand anything like the tens of millions of bullets armies routinely used in the course of the fighting. In the nineteenth century, war would become industrialized, with death, unhappily, mass-produced.

In the past, changes to weaponry came slowly; the gunpowder of Roger Bacon in the thirteenth century was not essentially different from the powder used in the American Revolution 500 years later; the flintlock remained in use for 200 years virtually unchanged. But in the 1800s changes would come thick and fast.

One important innovation was the general shift from muzzle to breech loading. As we have seen, breech loading had always been more convenient. The problem was to make a tight-fitting seal to the breech to keep gas from escaping and thus reducing the power of the explosion. Then, with better systems of working metal and especially the new machine tools, close-fitting breech devices could be manufactured. For artillerymen the shift to breech loading allowed them to stand behind some kind of cover while they worked. For infantrymen, breech loading allowed a soldier to load while kneeling, crouching, or even lying down, which was difficult to do with the old muzzle loader. Equally important was the development of superior recoil systems, which allowed the cannons to take up the shock without bouncing around as much as they had in the past.

An important factor in the change to breech loading was the advent of the fixed cartridge—the modern bullet as we know it—with the powder, primer, and projectile all contained in a brass case. A rudimentary type of cartridge was developed by a Swiss inventor named Samuel Johannes Pauly in 1812. Over the next few decades many types of cartridges were tried. The Civil War, in particular, gave impetus to the development of the cartridge. Most of these early cartridges were fired by a hammer that struck a pin. The pin in turn rammed into the base of the cartridge where a bit of primer was stored, thereby exploding it. By 1866 the metal cartridge, with its own primer fired by a pin, was fully developed. It remains in principle the same today.

The cartridge simplified the loading and storage of ammunition substantially. But a key point about the cartridge was that when the powder exploded, the brass shell expanded, forming a tight seal in the chamber, and thus helped to prevent gas from escaping from the breech.

As ever, one development opened the way for another. For centuries, almost from the time of the first guns, military experts have been trying to figure out a way to shoot a rapid series of bullets from a single weapon. Most of these efforts were based on the idea of bundling several gun barrels together so they could be fired simultaneously or in rapid succession. The first to have any success with this idea was American Samuel Colt. At sixteen, inspired by the revolving spokes on a ship's wheel, Colt conceived of the idea of the revolving barrel. In 1830 he whittled a model in wood, and in 1835 he had a working model ready. The principle was simple enough: a cylinder containing six chambers revolved so as to bring one chamber into position behind the gun barrel when the hammer was pulled back. When the trigger was pulled, the hammer fell, firing that chamber. The hammer was pulled back again and a new chamber revolved into place. Each chamber had to be loaded in advance and fitted with a percussion cap, but once the gun was loaded it could fire six shots very rapidly.

The principle could have been applied to a rifle, but Colt's gun was a pistol. He was sure that his six-shooter would find ready customers, but the U.S. government wasn't interested, and Colt's company quickly failed. Discouraged, he turned to other projects.

But some of Colt's six-shooters found their way west, where they were seized upon by westerners as a use-

Fig. 251.—The original Colt's Revolver.

THE COLT REVOLVER CONSTANTLY UNDERWENT IMPROVEMENT, BUT THE BASIC IDEA REMAINED THE SAME: THE CYLINDER TURNED FROM ONE CHAMBER TO THE NEXT WHEN THE HAMMER WAS RAISED, BRINGING A NEW CHARGE INTO POSITION. THIS IS THE ORIGINAL VERSION.

ful weapon for fighting Indians, robbers, and marauding animals. Soon a contingent of fifteen Texas Rangers, equipped with the Colt six-shooters, fought off a large party of Comanches, killing many of them. The weapon subsequently became very popular with the rangers. In 1847 when rangers were fighting in the Mexican War, other soldiers discovered it. Soon the government changed its mind and began issuing six-shooters to soldiers, especially the cavalry. Samuel Colt got back into the gun business and grew wealthy. The Colt six-shooter remains one of the great legends of the West.

A revolver such as the Colt had limited range and was not as accurate as a rifle. It was obvious that a repeating rifle would be an enormous advantage in war. In fact, as early as the seventeenth century, guns had been devised that could fire several shots in rapid succession. These weapons were fitted with magazines—storage chambers—into which balls and powder were loaded. Through a system of levers and gears a ball and powder were delivered to the chamber from the magazines. The mechanisms that worked repeating guns were very delicate. They had to be carefully maintained, jammed easily, and were expensive to make; thus, they were not practical for army use.

In fact only when cartridges became available was it really possible to make a repeating rifle. The cartridge allowed the bullet, primer, and powder to be loaded with one simple motion. The development of the repeating rifle was the work of many hands. The groundwork was laid by Walter Hunt, who has been called the archetype (model) of all impractical geniuses. In 1849 Hunt patented a repeater that worked on the same principles as later ones, but he never capitalized on it. Hunt's mechanism was also delicate, and over the next decade various inventors and mechanics tinkered with it, including Horace Smith and Daniel B. Wesson, who gave their names to one of America's best-known gun companies. Eventually the numerous patents for the weapon came under control of a businessman named Oliver F. Winchester. Further modifications were made, and in 1862 when the Civil War was under way, the repeating rifle was ready.

It was worked by a lever under the trigger, which moved mechanisms to withdraw the spent shell, push in a new one, and cock the gun in one rapid motion. With this gun, a shooter could fire at the rate of a shot every two or three seconds. It was excellent, but a conservative army chief refused to order more than a handful of the new repeaters. Only late in the war were repeaters used in any quantity. It is interesting to ponder how the war might have gone had the North equipped its troops with repeaters. In the end the weapon grew famous in the West as the gun of choice. The best-known brand was the Winchester: it became an American legend.

Yet repeaters, whether the Colt revolver or the Winchester rifle, could fire only a certain number of shots before they had to be reloaded. The ideal was to find a weapon that would fire continuously for a long period. The new cartridge, which could be loaded into the chamber in one motion, provided the answer. In 1862 an American, Richard Gatling, designed the Gatling gun, the first effective machine gun. The Gatling gun was similar to the Colt six-shooter in that it was built around the idea of revolving barrels. As each barrel revolved into place, a new bullet was inserted, ready to be fired in its turn. The machine gunner spun the barrels with a crank handle. The Gatling gun could fire up to 600 rounds per minute. It was used in the Civil War, but not enough of them were available before the end of the war to have a serious impact on the fighting.

Then in 1883 Hiram S. Maxim, an Englishman born in the United States, invented the Maxim gun which, in later versions, became the deadly machine gun used in the world wars of the twentieth century. Maxim abandoned the idea of revolving barrels or chambers, on which most schemes for rapid-fire weapons had previously been based. Instead his model used the recoil of the gun itself to power it. According to the basic laws of physics, when a gun is fired not only is the bullet impelled for-

AN EARLY VERSION OF THE GATLING GUN. THE CLUSTERED BARRELS REVOLVED AND WERE LOADED AND FIRED RAPIDLY IN TURN.

SIR HIRAM MAXIM WITH HIS MAXIM MACHINE GUN, THE PRECURSOR TO MODERN MACHINE GUNS, WHICH ACCORDING TO ONE AUTHORITY HAVE KILLED MORE SOLDIERS THAN ANY OTHER WEAPON. THE MAXIM GUN WAS FED FROM A BELT, WHICH RAN THROUGH THE CHAMBER.

ward, but the gun itself is shoved backward at the same time. With rifles, the shooter's shoulder prevents the gun from flying backward. With the Maxim gun the whole barrel was allowed to recoil backwards a short distance with each shot. This backward movement activated machinery that removed the spent shell from the chamber, inserted a fresh bullet, closed the breech, cocked the gun, and then fired it, all in one quick motion. The bullets were fed in by a belt, and the barrel, which would get red hot with so much firing, was cooled by a casing of water around it. Machine guns have been improved considerably since the days of the Maxim gun, but the underlying principle on which they work is the same. One military historian has said, "Probably no other type of weapon has killed so many soldiers."

The nineteenth century was a great age of technical innovation, feeding the Industrial Revolution, and in turn fed by it. Not surprisingly it was also a great age of science. Chemistry in particular was coming into its own in the late eighteenth century, and by about 1800 the basic principles of modern chemistry had been formulated. Inevitably scientists began to unravel the chemistry of explosives. This was not solely for military purposes. Explosives had been used in mining for some time. Then, as engineering and architecture advanced, heavy steel bridges and eventually steel-frame buildings were being built. These needed holes for foundations often set in rock, which could most easily be made by blasting. The boom in railroads during the mid-nineteenth century also created a need for explosives to help tunnel through, or around, mountains. The demand for high-powered, controllable explosives was quickly growing.

Nonetheless, the use of explosives for military purposes was on everybody's mind. Up until the nineteenth century, the old gunpowder of saltpeter, sulfur, and charcoal had changed little. The first major improvement was the discovery of what was called guncotton in 1845–1846 by a German scientist. Guncotton was produced by the action of various acids on cotton. For some time it proved to be very volatile and prone to go off accidentally. In 1865 Sir Frederick Abel discovered a way to make it stable, and ultimately it rose in popularity as "smokeless powder" because it did not burn with the black fumes in the same way as the old gunpowder.

A second major new explosive was nitroglycerin, which was discovered in 1846. In 1862 a Swede, Alfred Nobel, began to manufacture nitroglycerin on a large scale. It too proved volatile: in 1864 an explosion in his factory killed his brother and gave his father a paralytic stroke. However, Nobel pressed on, and in 1867 he worked out a way to make nitroglycerin more stable and created one of the most famous of all modern explosives, dynamite. Nobel himself was disheartened by the extent to which his invention was used to slaughter other humans, and he soon established the Nobel Peace Prize, given annually to someone who advances the cause of peace in the world.

Chemistry had thus improved gunpowder, making it safer and more powerful—and making warfare just that much more deadly. The effects were felt at sea as well as on land. As we have seen, guns were placed on ships as early as the fifteenth century and perhaps earlier. Over time, as naval vessels grew larger, they were equipped with more and more cannons, some of them in two ranks down each side of the warship. Commercial vessels too began to carry a few cannons for defense against pirates or hostile people they might meet in their far-ranging trips.

The tactics used in naval battles were complex. The idea was to maneuver your ships into position where they could sweep the enemy ships with a "broadside," which in turn meant skillful use of the wind. If cannon fire could bring down enemy sails and masts, the ship would sit helpless in the water and might then be captured. However, during battles naval vessels often caught fire and burned to the waterline or were sunk because of holes in the hull.

In the 1820s the French developed the idea of using shells against wooden-hulled naval vessels. Exploding shells had been in use previously, but had not been used much on ships because they too frequently exploded accidentally. As safer types were developed, other navies followed the French example. In order to defend against shells, they began sheathing their ships in sheets of thick iron, much like the old armor of the mounted knights. At the same time, the rotating gun turret was developed, which could swivel all the way around so it could shoot in any direction no matter where the ship was facing. In 1862, during the Civil War, Union and Confederate ironclad ships met off the coast of Virginia in the celebrated battle of the *Monitor* and the *Merrimac*. The shells of each ship bounced off the iron armor of the other, and the fight ended in a draw. But the day of the wooden fighting ship was over; from then on naval vessels would be made of iron and steel.

The day of wind too was over. Steam-driven ships, at first meant for use on rivers and lakes, had been invented in the late 1700s. By the early nineteenth century the famous steam-powered paddle wheelers were pushing in droves up the Mississippi, the Hudson, the Ohio, and other rivers, and across the Great Lakes. For a relatively brief heyday, until the railroads outdid them, steamers were an important part of the American transportation system.

By the 1840s the screw propeller, the kind used today on small outboard motors as well as on giant aircraft carriers, came into use. Steam-powered ships using screw propellers rapidly took over the oceangoing trade, both for military and commercial uses. By the end of the nineteenth century, naval vessels had assumed the shape they would continue to have through the twentieth century: steel-hulled ships with revolving gun turrets and a screw propeller.

With these new weapons—the machine gun and the repeating rifle, ever-more powerful cannons, faster ships equipped with more deadly guns—the firepower of armies had increased beyond the imaginings of the men who had fought the American Civil War, many of whom were still alive. By 1900 a battery of machine guns could shoot more lead in an hour than whole armies could have two centuries earlier. The groundwork for the deadliest of all wars, the two world wars of the twentieth century, had been laid.

During recent wars the U.S. military has often sent combat artists into battle to make paintings of the action. Usually the artists made quick sketches on the spot and then completed full paintings later. This painting, by George Harding, shows soldiers attacking with the support of tanks. Tanks played a significant role late in World War II in bringing about the Allied victory.

SEVEN

The Bloody Century

World War I should never have happened, and once started, it should never have been allowed to develop as it did. It is true of course that many, if not most wars, are caused by human ambition, greed, or the belief in a certain cause, and should not have happened. But World War I is a particularly egregious example.

In 1900, as was frequently the case, Europe was beset by a complex web of alliances and rivalries. Various countries had signed treaties requiring them to come to the aid of others if attacked. The once-powerful Austro-Hungarian Empire had fallen from glory, but remained a force in European politics. In 1908 the empire annexed the small Balkan principality of Bosnia without bothering even to offer a good excuse. Neighboring Serbia saw this as a challenge, and there developed in Serbia a good deal of bitterness toward Austro-Hungary. In June 1914 the Archduke Ferdinand of Austria foolishly paid a state visit to Sarajevo, Bosnia's capital. There he was assassinated. Austria used the murder as an excuse to make demands on Serbia. Russia rushed to the defense of Serbia. The terms of some of those former treaties now came into play, and the turmoil began.

In fact, had the leaders of the major nations seriously wanted to keep the peace, they could have renegotiated and gotten around the treaties.

But some of them were spoiling for a fight. More than forty years earlier, France had lost a war to Germany and wanted revenge; Germany wanted to enlarge its eastern borders; other nations had their own sets of fears and ambitions. By August 1914 the British, Russians, and French were lined up against the Germans and Austrians. Eventually other nations would enter the fight. World War I had begun.

The Germans raced into Belgium and France and came close to capturing Paris. But the British and French held firm, and by winter the two sides were facing each other in a long line of trenches that ran through France and Belgium from the sea almost to the German border. Over most of the next four years, the vast armies, comprising millions of men, wrestled back and forth along this line, neither side ever able to advance more than fifty miles (eighty kilometers), despite even the bloodiest of fighting. In most cases "victories" were measured in yards.

The soldiers lived, fought, and died in their trenches and the "no-man's-land" between them. Trenches were deep and in some areas were outfitted with elaborate shelters made of wood or dug into trench walls. During times of quiet, the troops might live in a little comfort.

But mostly they did not. It seemed to many of the soldiers that it rained steadily for the four years of the war. There was mud everywhere—mud in the trenches, in no-man's-land, behind the lines. The soldiers stood guard on their stands in the trenches in cold, drizzling rain, soaked through their clothes. Then after weeks of routine patrols, they would be given the order to attack. They would wait in the trenches while their artillery pounded the enemy hour after hour. Then they would go over the top to stumble through mud, tripping over stumps of broken trees, falling into shell holes, through a torrent of machine-gun fire, only to be greeted by heavy strands of barbed wire, which might catch them and hold them fast while machine guns raked their bodies. Perhaps they would, in the end, reach the enemy trenches, where they would fight with hand grenades, clubs, or bayonets. More often they would be forced to retreat, leaving their friends dead or dying in no-man's-land with nothing gained.

Defending against an attack was a little less dangerous. However, an attack was usually preceded by an intense bombardment with high-explosive shells. Soldiers would crouch in the dugouts, knowing that at any moment they were likely to be blown to bits or buried alive, the harrowing noise driving into their ears.

Inevitably the loss of life was staggering. In the battle of the Somme River, in France, which lasted from July 1 until November 18, 1916, half a million men were killed, wounded, or taken prisoner; out of the bloodshed, the French and British gained nine miles (fourteen kilometers). The ten-month battle for the town of Verdun, also in France, was even worse: 420,000 died while 800,000 were gassed or wounded. At the end of it all, the lines were precisely where they had started.

ANOTHER OF GEORGE HARDING'S COMBAT PAINTINGS SHOWS SOLDIERS WEARING GAS MASKS. GAS WAS A TERRIBLE WEAPON, GREATLY FEARED BY SOLDIERS. IT WAS EVENTUALLY BANNED FROM USE IN WAR, DISCONTINUED BECAUSE IT WAS SO DIFFICULT TO CONTROL.

The lesson still had not been learned. With modern firepower, a relatively small number of well-dug-in defenders could stop a much larger attacking force. When the numbers of attackers and defenders were anything like equal, an attack was hopeless. But nobody could figure out anything better to do than to throw brave soldiers at each other.

One weapon heavily responsible for the awful death toll was the recently developed machine gun. It is true of course that before World War I nobody had seen what concentrations of machine-gun fire could do in a major battle, and at first its importance was underestimated. At the start of the war, the British had two machine guns per infantry battalion; by the end of the war, there were whole battalions of machine gunners in the trenches.

A second deadly new weapon was poison gas: World War I was the only major conflict in which gas was used. There were several types, but perhaps the most feared was mustard gas, because it tore at your lungs, choking you. If you survived, your lungs might be permanently damaged.

Another new weapon was the airplane. The small fragile planes of the time were not capable of doing any significant bombing. They were, however, useful for observation, especially to help guide artillery to their targets. They would become vital weapons only in the next world war.

Much more significant was the submarine. During the American Civil War the Confederacy had developed some small underwater vessels that had done damage to Northern shipping. Interest in the idea of submersible ships was slow to develop, but in the years leading up to World War I the concept attracted more attention. By 1914 both the British and the Germans had small fleets of subs equipped with torpedoes filled with TNT and propelled by compressed air.

The Germans made the most use of subs, much of it against American shipping. The majority of Americans were determined to stay out of the war, which they believed was not their business. However, as the fighting went on, they supported the British and French more and more. Americans began selling large quantities of food, weapons, and other necessities to the combatants, but especially to the British. The Germans needed to choke off this stream of goods flowing across the Atlantic into the British

Isles, and in time they started attacking American merchant ships. Had the Germans been able to stop the flood of supplies coming into England they probably could have won the war. However, the British eventually worked out the convoy system, in which merchant vessels traveled in groups protected by warships. A few of the ships might be sunk, but most of them managed to get through. Merchant-ship losses fell dramatically.

Like the airplane, the tank played only a minor role in World War I, but would be of major importance in World War II. In 1914 the automobile, built around the internal-combustion gasoline engine, was just beginning to come into widespread use; as late as 1914 only a small minority of American families owned cars. However armies had begun to switch from horse-drawn wagons to trucks, and as the war progressed, trucks and motorized ambulances took over in rear areas, although horses remained in use right through the war.

It occurred to several people that a heavily armored truck might be the answer to barbed wire and machine guns, but it was the British who first produced a practical tank and rolled it out onto the battlefields in 1916. The tank finally showed what it could do in the battle for Cambrai, France, in November 1917. Without any initial bombardment, 300 British tanks led the infantry forward into no-man's-land. The tanks crashed through the barbed wire, chased off the machine gunners, and slashed a hole 4 miles (6.4 km) wide. The British took 10,000 German prisoners.

Slowly the lesson was being learned. An Australian general, John Monash said, "The true role of infantry was not . . . to wither away under merciless machine-gun fire . . . but to advance under maximum protection of . . . guns, machine-guns, tanks, mortars and aeroplanes." The British stepped up production of tanks. On August 8, 1918, they mounted a massive attack at Amiens with tanks, infantry, and some air support. Before the morning was over, some units had gained 7 miles (11.3 km), more than many previous attacks had gained after months of fighting. After the Amiens battle, a top German official called it, "The black day of the German Army in the history of war." In November the Germans asked for peace.

The tank alone did not end World War I. The Americans had come into the war in 1917, mainly out of anger over German sub attacks on American ships, and while it took time for them to become a significant force in the war, they helped to tip the balance. Moreover, German resistance was finally collapsing, and morale was breaking down. As one historian has said, they "had had enough."

In the end, World War I, despite the horrendous bloodletting, accomplished little. Once again the human failings of stupidity, greed, and the desire for revenge left matters unresolved. Many historians today are inclined to see World War II as a continuation of World War I.

Part of the problem was that the French, who had been humiliated by the Germans in the Franco-Prussian War some fifty years earlier, wanted to see Germany ruined as a major power. They insisted on harsh terms in the peace treaty. Inevitably the Germans, unwilling to accept their defeat, grew bitter and ached for revenge.

Another part of the trouble was the economic downturn that began in the 1920s and worsened through the worldwide depression of the 1930s. Germany, still struggling to get out from under the problems caused by the World War I, was badly hit by the economic downturn. When a forceful new leader appeared, promising to return Germany to its rightful place as a great nation, the Germans succumbed to his will. That leader was, of course, Adolf Hitler.

Once in office, Hitler's Nazi party assumed absolute power through oppressive measures, including torture and execution of those who opposed it. Contrary to the terms of the peace treaty, Hitler rebuilt Germany's armed forces, and step by step began swallowing up its smaller neighbors. The British and the French, with no stomach for another bloody war, gave in again and again. Finally, when Hitler marched into Poland in 1939 after promising that he wouldn't, the British and French had to act, and World War II was on.

Once again this war was far too extensive to discuss in a few pages. It spread across the globe, with heavy fighting in Europe, North Africa, the Pacific Ocean, China and other places in Asia. It has been called a total war, because not only soldiers, but millions of civilians were killed or wounded in it, due to the shelling and bombing of cities. Perhaps 40 million people died, although nobody is sure of the exact figure.

Most significantly, by the time of World War II, other areas of the world had caught up technologically with the Europeans and Americans. In the 1920s and even earlier, the Chinese, tired of being at the mercy of the West, had begun modernizing their army. Other nations were doing the same. In particular Japan, which had maintained a militaristic tradition for a long time, had with astonishing rapidity built itself a huge fighting force based on Western models.

Japan had long resented Western power and influence in Asia. It believed that Japan, not the Western nations, ought to control the areas surrounding its home islands. By the late 1930s it had a substantial fleet of modern warships, including many aircraft carriers; a large air force with excellent planes, such as its "Zero" fighters; and a large army. Japan was ready for war.

Once again the Americans wanted to stay out of the war. Some, among them President Franklin D. Roosevelt, felt that the United States had to join the effort to stop Hitler and his Italian ally, the dictator Benito Mussolini. But although public opinion mainly supported the French and British against the dictators, Americans still remembered the slaughterhouse of no-man's-land and wanted to remain on the sidelines.

Then, on the famous date of December 7, 1941, the Japanese launched a surprise attack against Western outposts in Asia—British colonies such as Singapore, Dutch ones in what is now Indonesia, and American ones in the Philippines. In particular, Japanese bombers caught many ships of the American fleet in its base at Pearl Harbor, Hawaii, and destroyed both ships and planes at nearby air bases. The United States was then dragged into the war.

World War II has been called the last good war. By this, people mean that the Allies, essentially, the Americans, Russians, and the British and their dominions such as Australia and Canada, were poised against the totalitarian governments of the Axis—Germany, Italy, and Japan. (France surrendered early in the war, and the Chinese were fully engaged in fighting the Japanese in their own country.) The Axis powers were, by their own admission, determined to take over as much of the world as they could, and spread their dictatorial ideas. Thus, by any reasonable definition, the Allies were morally right, the Axis powers wrong. In fact it would turn out that the Soviet Union, as Russia was then known, was just as dictatorial as the Axis powers. It is also hard to see why the Westerners had any more right, in principle, than the Japanese to be influential in other Asian nations. At bottom, however, the Axis powers intended to enslave other nations, and the Americans and British at least did not.

Over the four years after America's entry into the war until the end in August 1945, many bloody battles were fought in Europe, North Africa, Russia, much of Southeast Asia, China, and the Pacific Islands. Japan was bombed, but surrendered before it could be invaded, and there was lesser fighting elsewhere.

As far as weapons are concerned, most of the ones used in World War I were still important. Tanks were now routinely dispatched in support of infantry everywhere they could reasonably go. In the deserts of North Africa, the war was largely fought by tanks. Machine guns were a major weapon. Submarines circled the globe, sinking both merchant and warships. Only poisoned gas was not used, partly in fear of retaliation, partly because it was hard to control.

In any case, by now the lesson had been learned. Commanders were reluctant to throw masses of infantry against well-dug-in defenders. Every effort was made to soften up defenses with artillery and aerial bombardment first, and whenever possible, tanks were sent in with the infantry. Nonetheless, often in the end there was no other way but to send the infantry in. This was particularly true in the conquest by Americans of the little "stepping stone" islands across the Pacific heading toward Japan: eventually foot soldiers had to jump out of landing barges and slog across open water into heavy fire. Japanese defenders mostly managed to survive the initial bombardments, and the American death toll during these landings was always high.

World War II advanced the use of two major new weapons. One was the airplane. People had been trying to figure out a way to fly for millennia, and by the 1890s several people were close to success in France, the United States, and elsewhere. Credit for the first flight is generally given to

AIR POWER PROVED DECISIVE IN WORLD WAR II. THIS PAINTING BY A GERMAN ARTIST SHOWS AN ALLIED BOMBING ATTACK ON THE GERMAN CITY OF HAMBURG. THE PAINTING WAS SEIZED BY AMERICAN TROOPS AT THE END OF THE WAR.

the Wright brothers, who got a plane off the ground briefly at Kitty Hawk, North Carolina, in 1903, although there are other claimants as well. The military potential of flight was quickly seen, and by the 1920s many nations were developing air forces. Hitler, in his attacks on Poland, used dive-bombers to terrorize troops and fleeing refugees as well.

But more important were the huge fleets of bombers that all of the combatants used against fortifications and enemy cities. Over the course of the war, all of the nations involved did severe damage to enemy cities by bombing. Particularly important was the so-called Battle of Britain in 1940, when the Germans tried to bomb England out of the war by destroying its manufacturing capacity and breaking its morale. Failing that, Hitler hoped to eliminate the British air force to open the way for an invasion of

AT SEA, THE AIRCRAFT CARRIER REPLACED THE BATTLESHIP AS THE MOST IMPORTANT MEMBER OF THE FLEET. HERE PLANES ARE LAUNCHED FROM A CARRIER FLIGHT DECK FOR A PATROL AT DAWN.

the British Isles. The effort failed: the British air force was able to shoot down enough of the German bombers to discourage the effort, and Britain was never invaded.

But while mass bombing was sometimes used to break civilian morale, it was also used against enemy factories, railroad yards, dams, power plants, and oil fields in order to destroy the enemy's productive capacity. At the time, it appeared that these raids were causing great damage. A more careful look suggests that even countries that were heavily bombed usually managed to make repairs fairly quickly. Despite severe bombings, many German factories were operating right up to that country's surrender.

There were two defenses against bombers. One was antiaircraft guns, aided at night by powerful searchlights, which proved to be very effective against massed bombers—so much so, that in time the Allied bombing of Germany was frequently carried out at night or from high altitudes. The second defense consisted of fast, maneuverable fighter planes such as the British Spitfire and the German Messerschmitt 109. These planes could easily shoot down much slower bombers, but in turn they were vulnerable to the bomber's machine guns, or to fighters protecting the bombers, which provided cover when the bombers were not traveling too far.

Air power proved to be equally important at sea. The Japanese victory at Pearl Harbor was mainly due to planes launched from aircraft carriers. But the Americans got their revenge at the Battle of Midway. They had cracked the Japanese radio code and knew that the Japanese wanted to destroy the American base on Midway Island, not far from Hawaii, at a point the early sea captains believed to be roughly midway across the Pacific. Knowing what the Japanese were up to, the Americans caught them in the open seas, and their dive-bombers hit them hard. Within a few minutes, three of four Japanese carriers were in flames, their bombs exploding on their decks. In that few minutes the Japanese naval effort was crippled. Sea battles such as Midway showed that the day of the heavy battleship was over. From then on, aircraft from carriers would be essential naval vessels. In modern wars, carriers are used against armies on land as well as against naval vessels.

The second great new weapon to appear in World War II was, of course, the atomic bomb. For some time, scientists had realized that the force holding the parts of an atom together was extremely strong and could be used for energy if a way could be found to release it. The great scientist Albert Einstein worked out a formula for this binding force, $E = mc^2$. When World War II began, some American scientists, fearful that the Germans might be working on an atomic bomb, asked Einstein to sign a letter to President Roosevelt suggesting that the government develop such a weapon before the Germans could. Roosevelt authorized the very secret Manhattan Project to build an atomic bomb, and in the summer of 1945 one was successfully tested.

By this time the Germans and Italians had been defeated in Europe, but the Japanese were still fighting a tough and bloody war in the Pacific. President Harry S Truman, who had succeeded Roosevelt, agreed that the bomb should be used. The first atomic bomb was dropped on Hiroshima, a major Japanese city, obliterating the center of the city and killing tens of thousands of people. When the Japanese did not immediately surrender, another bomb was dropped on the city of Nagasaki, with similar results. This time the Japanese agreed to surrender, and World War II was over.

Ever since, there have been debates over the morality of using the bomb. Many have believed then and now, that far more people—Japanese as well as Americans—would have died if the bomb had not been used and the war had gone on. The Japanese, although losing, were defending to the death every stepping-stone island, and an invasion of Japan itself would have been tremendously costly in human life for both sides. Others argued that the Japanese might have been persuaded to surrender sooner or later anyway. Whatever the case, the feeling in the United States was strong against the Japanese, who had shown little mercy to others throughout the war. Americans at the time felt that the Japanese had gotten what they deserved. The attitude was that no more American soldiers ought to die to spare the Japanese the atomic bomb. It is a subject worth debating.

However, ever since, nobody anywhere has used the atomic bomb or its more powerful successors. Most people realize that any country that uses the bomb is bound to be bombed back. There has thus come about a sys-

To reach Japan, the Americans landed on a series of Pacific island "stepping stones." These beach assaults were very bloody and costly in human lives. Here Americans land on Arawe, New Britain.

tem of mutual deterrence: no country, no matter how powerful, dares to use a nuclear bomb, for fear of retaliation. The nuclear bomb, then, is really the ultimate weapon, as far as explosives are concerned: there is no point in producing anything more powerful, for a nuclear war could end civilization, and possibly life on Earth as well.

THE EVOLUTION OF WARFARE CAN BE SUMMARIZED IN THIS IMAGE OF A WORLD WAR II BOMBER FLYING OVER BARNWELL CASTLE IN ENGLAND, ON ITS WAY TO TARGETS IN GERMANY. WAR WAS ALWAYS DEADLY, BUT TODAY THE INSTRUMENTS OF DEATH ARE FAR MORE POWERFUL THAN AT THE TIME BARNWELL CASTLE WAS BUILT.

EIGHT

What Does It All Mean?

It was roughly a thousand years between the invention of gunpowder and the dropping of the atomic bomb. Human beings have shown themselves to be very clever at devising machines for slaughtering each other. They have not shown themselves to be nearly as clever at keeping themselves from using those machines. Over and over again people of good will have tried to work out schemes for bringing peace to Earth. Indeed, peace is a major goal of many of the world's religions. Many efforts have been made to limit the types of weapons that can be used in war. As far back as 1139 the Roman Catholic Church forbade the use of the crossbow as too murderous for "Christian warfare." Three centuries later many people truly believed that gunpowder was the invention of the devil, a conviction that continued for many centuries. In the sixteenth century, wheel locks were banned in several cities, viewed as too dangerous a weapon. The invention of the percussion cap caused another outcry. One writer said that with it "war would shortly become so frightful as to exceed all bounds of imagination. Future wars would threaten, within a few years, to destroy not only armies, but civilization itself." The same was thought of exploding bullets, which were first tried in the Civil War. General Grant said, "Their use is barbarous, because they produce increased suffering without any increased advantage to those using them." A conference of nations agreed, outlawing their use. Then after World War I, it was agreed that poison gas should be outlawed as unnecessarily cruel. More recently, efforts have been made to eliminate the use of hidden mines, which go on killing or maiming innocent people long after the fighting is over. Arms control is hardly a new idea.

Unfortunately, arms-control laws and agreements have usually been ignored, except when military leaders lose interest in a weapon. The crossbow was phased out only when the more effective gun was invented. The use of poison gas stopped when it was realized that it invited being attacked by the same means. The exploding bullet was dropped because it afforded no military advantage. Nuclear weapons have not been used because of the threat of retaliation.

Is there any hope that weapons can be controlled? To go further, is there any possibility that war itself might cease to exist? It does seem that many people have drawn a lesson from the immense slaughter of the world wars of the last century, that at least large-scale conflicts have to be avoided at all costs. World War I snuffed out much of the generation of young European men, leaving millions of parents without sons, wives without husbands, children without fathers. The story was much the same for some nations after World War II: the Russians alone lost possibly 20 million people. In that country millions of women lived on without husbands and children because so many of the men of their generations died in battle.

Thus, it continues to be important for us to read about wars and weapons—the crossbow, gunpowder, the vast slaughter in the trenches, and the mass bombing of cities. If we feel that it is necessary to fight, we must know the cost and be prepared to pay it. We must not be optimists like the ones who believed that the Civil War or World War I would be over in months. We must understand, as Shakespeare did, that when the dogs of war are loosed, there is no telling whom they may bite.

WEB SITES AND OTHER INFORMATION

Armor and Weapons
http://www.historyforkids.org/greekciv/war/army/seanh8.htm

Medieval Weapons Links
http://cybersleuth-kids.com/sleuth/History/Medieval/Medieval_Weapons/

Weapons through Time
http://www.bbc.co.uk/history/games/weapons/index.shtml

To contact the **National Muzzle Loading Rifle Association**, write to them at:
P.O. Box 67
Friendship, Indiana 47021

Bibliography

FOR STUDENTS
Blumenson, Martin, and James L. Stokesbury. *Masters of the Art of Command.* New York: Da Capo Press, 1990.

The Diagram Group, Davis Harding, and Jefferson Cann, eds. *Weapons: An International Encyclopedia from 5000 B.C. to 2000 A.D.* New York: St. Martin's Press, 1991.

Dupuy, Trevor N. *Evolution of Weapons and Warfare.* New York: Da Capo Press, 1984.

Fuller, J. F. C. *Armament and History.* New York: Da Capo Press, 1998.

FOR TEACHERS OR ADVANCED READERS
Black, Jeremy. *War and the World: Military Power and the Fate of Continents, 1450–2000.* New Haven, CT: Yale University Press, 1998.

Creasy, Edward S. *Fifteen Decisive Battles of the World: From Maryland to Waterloo.* New York: Da Capo Press, 1994.

Hanson, Victor Davis. *Carnage and Culture: Landmark Battles in the Rise of Western Power.* New York: Doubleday, 2001.

Index

Page numbers for illustrations are in **boldface.**

About the Author

James Lincoln Collier has written books for both adults and students on many subjects, among them the prizewinning novel *My Brother Sam Is Dead*. Many of these books, both fiction and nonfiction, have historical themes, including the highly acclaimed Benchmark Books series the Drama of American History, which he wrote with Christopher Collier.